Hello
I'm Feireina

I mostly go around as Fei and I'm a small artist trying to keep up with the economy.

Thank you so much for purchasing this little booklet of mine! I still can't believe I managed to finish inktober this year, it has been a huge journey of ups and downs.

The illustrations started getting a bit spicy towards the end, but I hope you still enjoy them!

There's also a coloring book version of this challenge. If you want to buy them as a book, they're available on my amazon, but if you want the PNG to colour digitally, feel free to check out my patreon shop!

SPECIAL THANKS

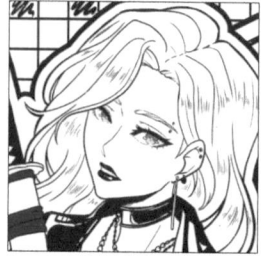

20   Goldenpeel

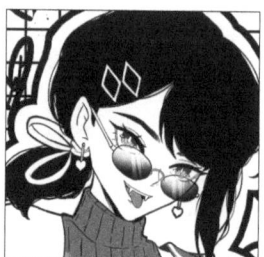

22   NymerianT

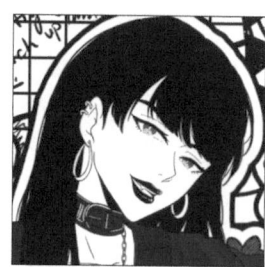

24   jamesmakan

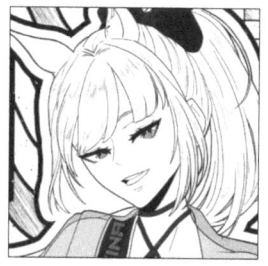

26   z33k1n

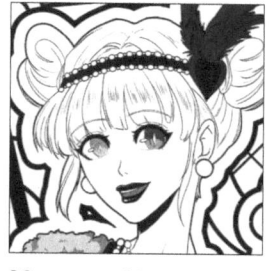

28   MoonAbsorb

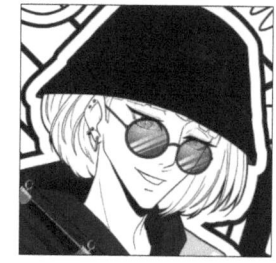

30   robek_world

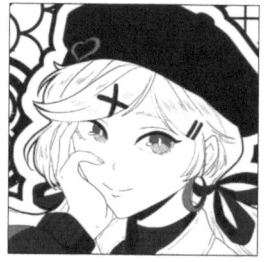

32   sai7

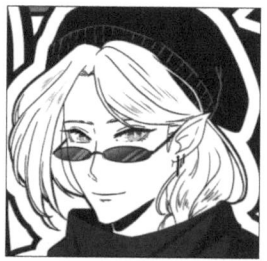

34   Vanaric

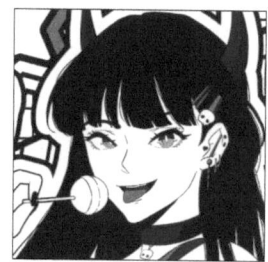

36   ligaratus_

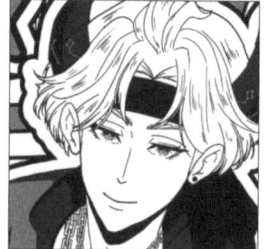

38   LooYiRen1

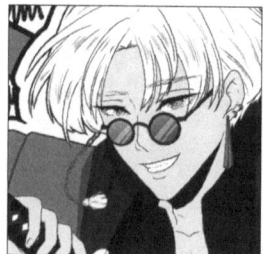

40   datdegenboi

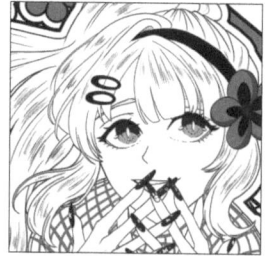

42   stxnezi

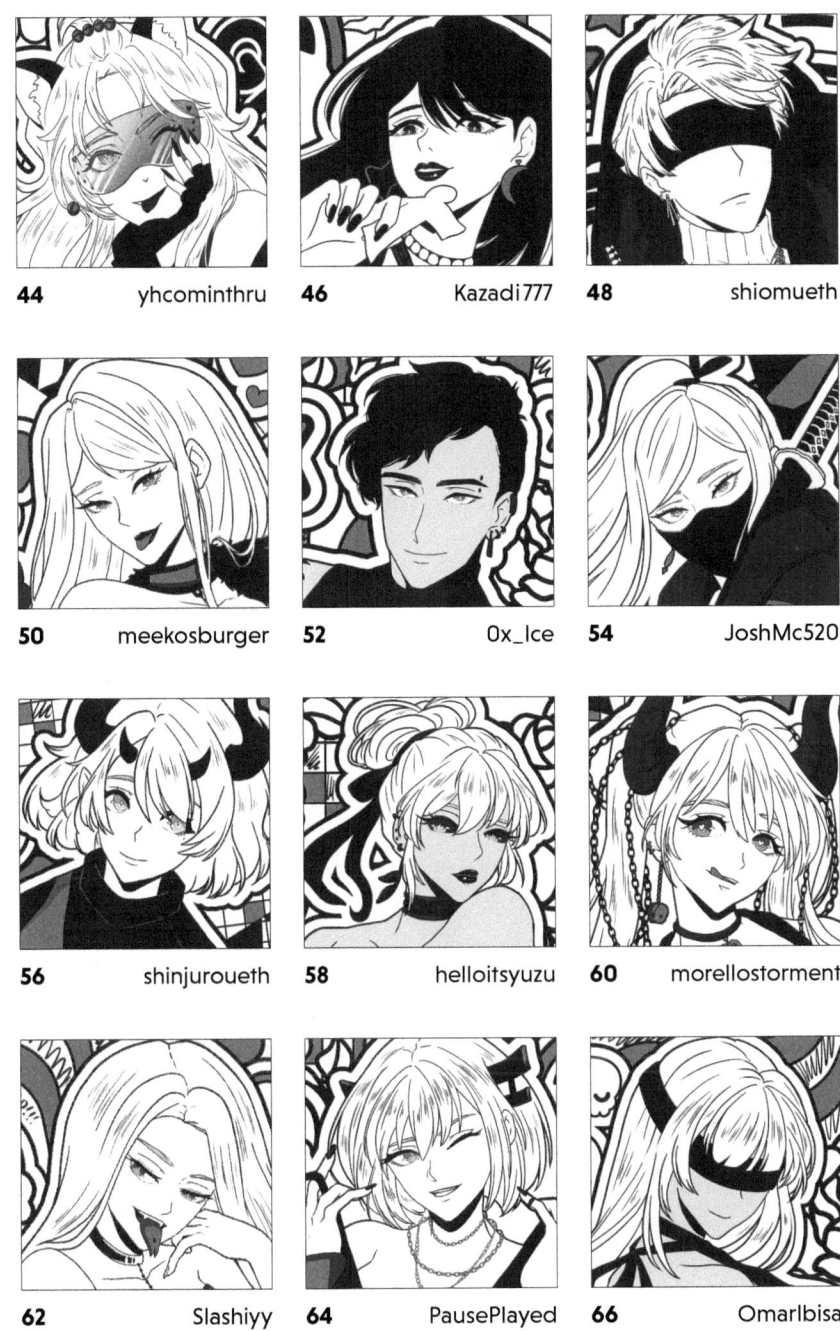

44   yhcominthru   **46**   Kazadi777   **48**   shiomueth

50   meekosburger   **52**   0x_Ice   **54**   JoshMc520

56   shinjuroueth   **58**   helloitsyuzu   **60**   morellostorment

62   Slashiyy   **64**   PausePlayed   **66**   OmarIbisa

Re- What?

This is where it all started, with my character Noah. You might be wondering, why am I seeing two of the same character?

Well, that was because the first one was the very first submission! The second one was redone to match the other inktobers. Once you flip through this book, you will notice the stark difference between this and the rest.

The text in the background says "Are you ready?" but it got covered by the character.

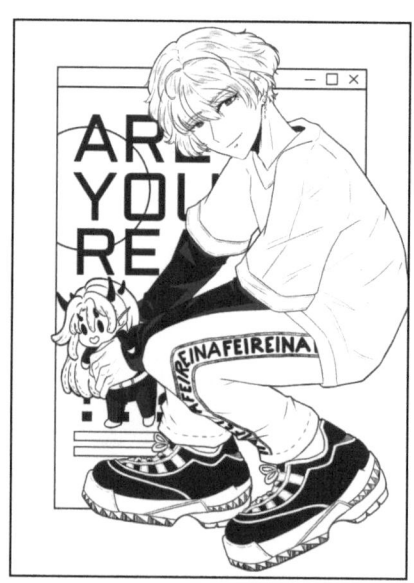

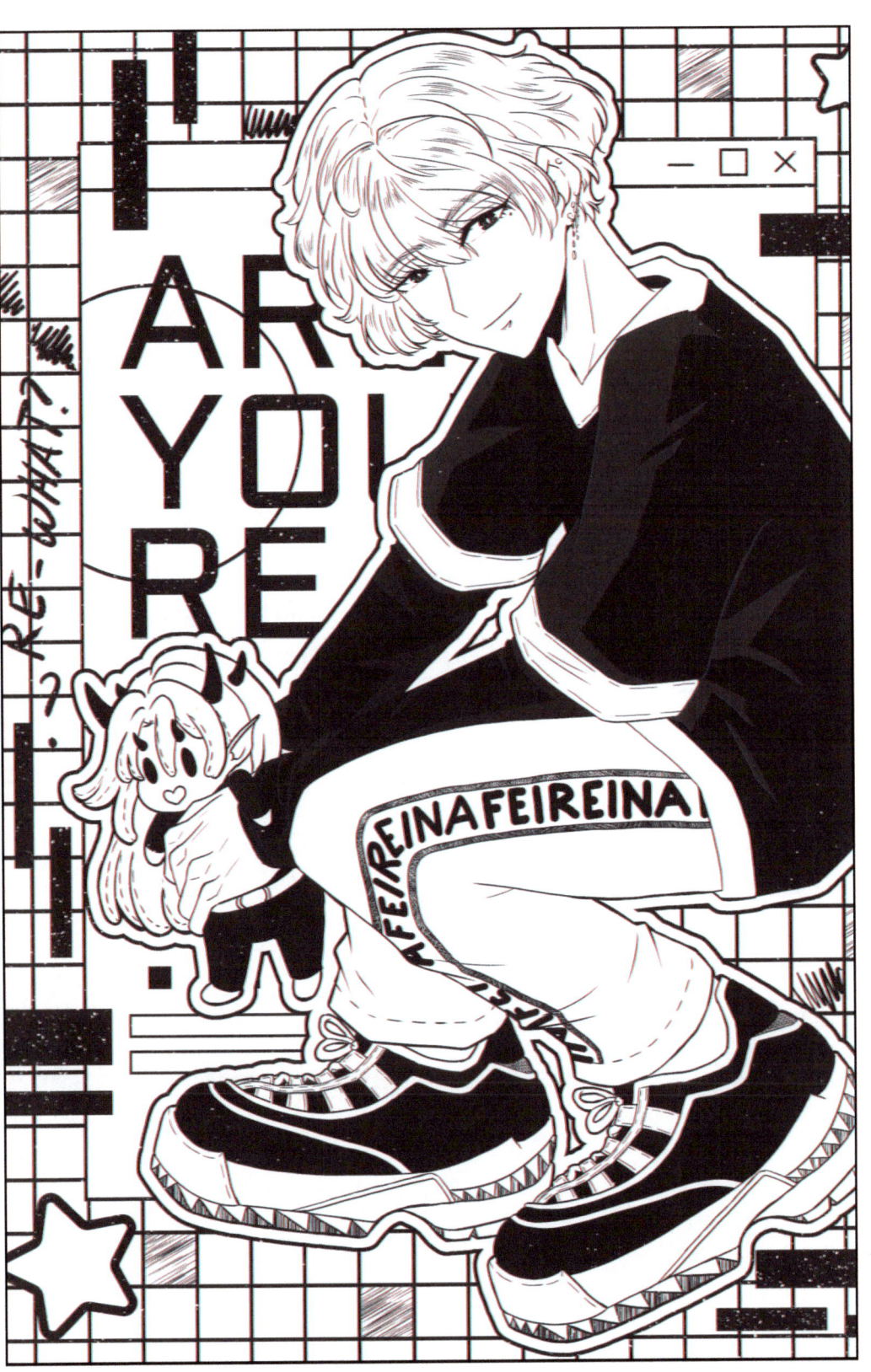

I need sleep

This is my character Rorie! She's Noah's twin sister and also the reason why the aesthetic of the inktober challenge took a huge turn from being very simple to more complicated.

There's not much to say about this piece aside from the fact that I wrote that "Love" text myself. It took a couple tries for it to come this smooth!

Originally, this book was only going to be a collection you can flip through, but I thought that it might be boring for you, my dearest reader, hence why I decided to add some word vomit over here.

Of course, it's not complete word vomitt, because if it was, there would be a lot of "lol"s and "hahas" at the end of the sentences instead of proper punctuation marks.

Even now, as I'm writing this I have to refrain from typing a "lol" at the end.

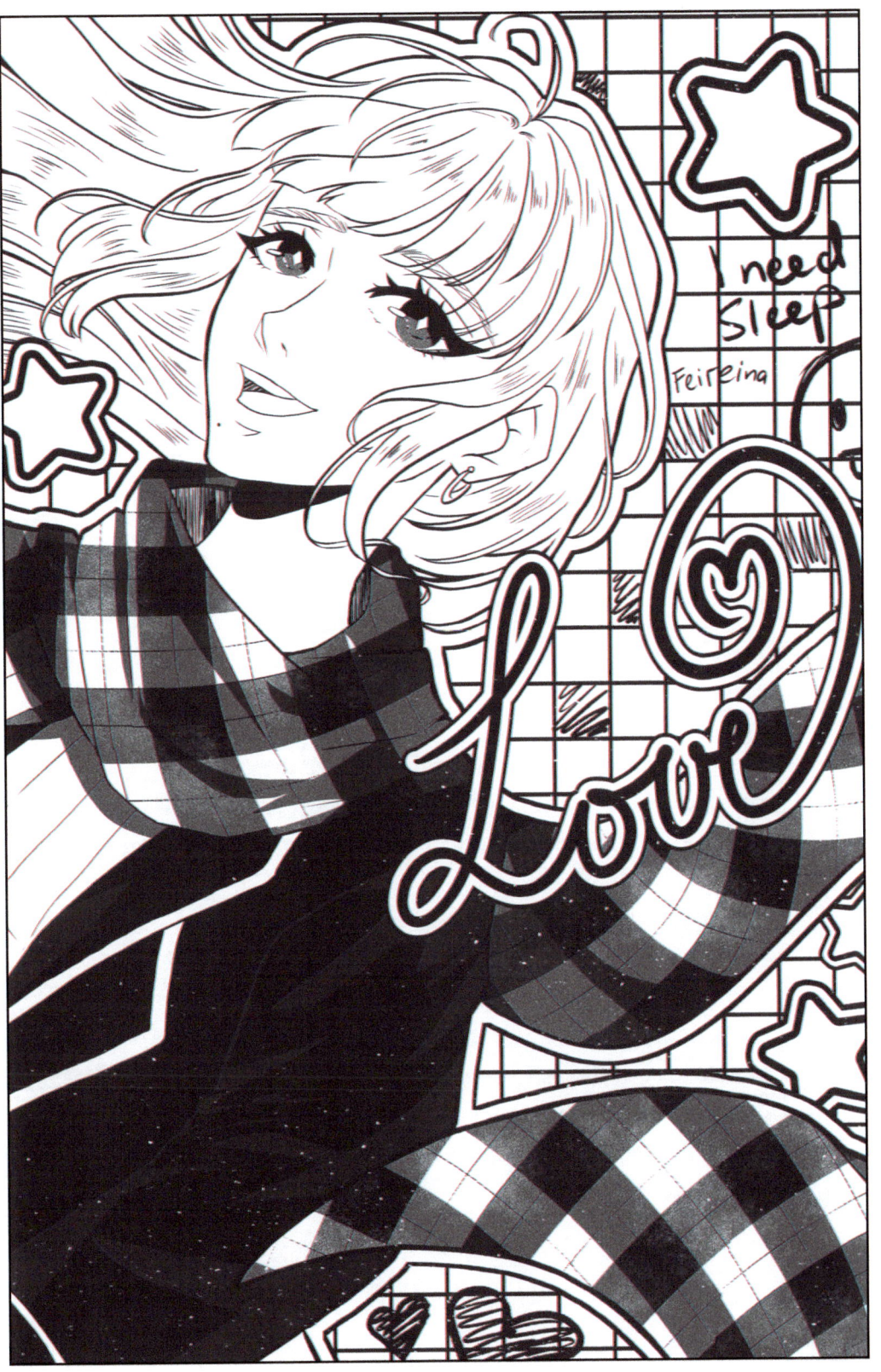

Bleh

WOWIE A GUN AMURICA KAWWW KAWWW lol

I let out enough cringe with this one page alone. I think I can be serious again (spoiler alert: I won't). All jokes aside, this is my OC Nomusa! She's probably one of my favourite OC's to illustrate aside from my twins Rorie and Noah.

I actually have a theme for each inktober piece, can you guess the theme for this one here? I think you've noticed by now, but I'm not following the official inktober prompts.

Why? Because I don't want to.

This illustration was really hard for me to draw and no, it's not because of the gun. That was the easy part because I just used a free 3d model from Clip Studio to get it right from the start.

What was hard was her left arm.

I had no idea what to do with it! So after trying several sketches for an hour, I just decided to hide it. What they don't know won't hurt them and all that. Except now you know because you're reading this. Let's keep it a secret okay?

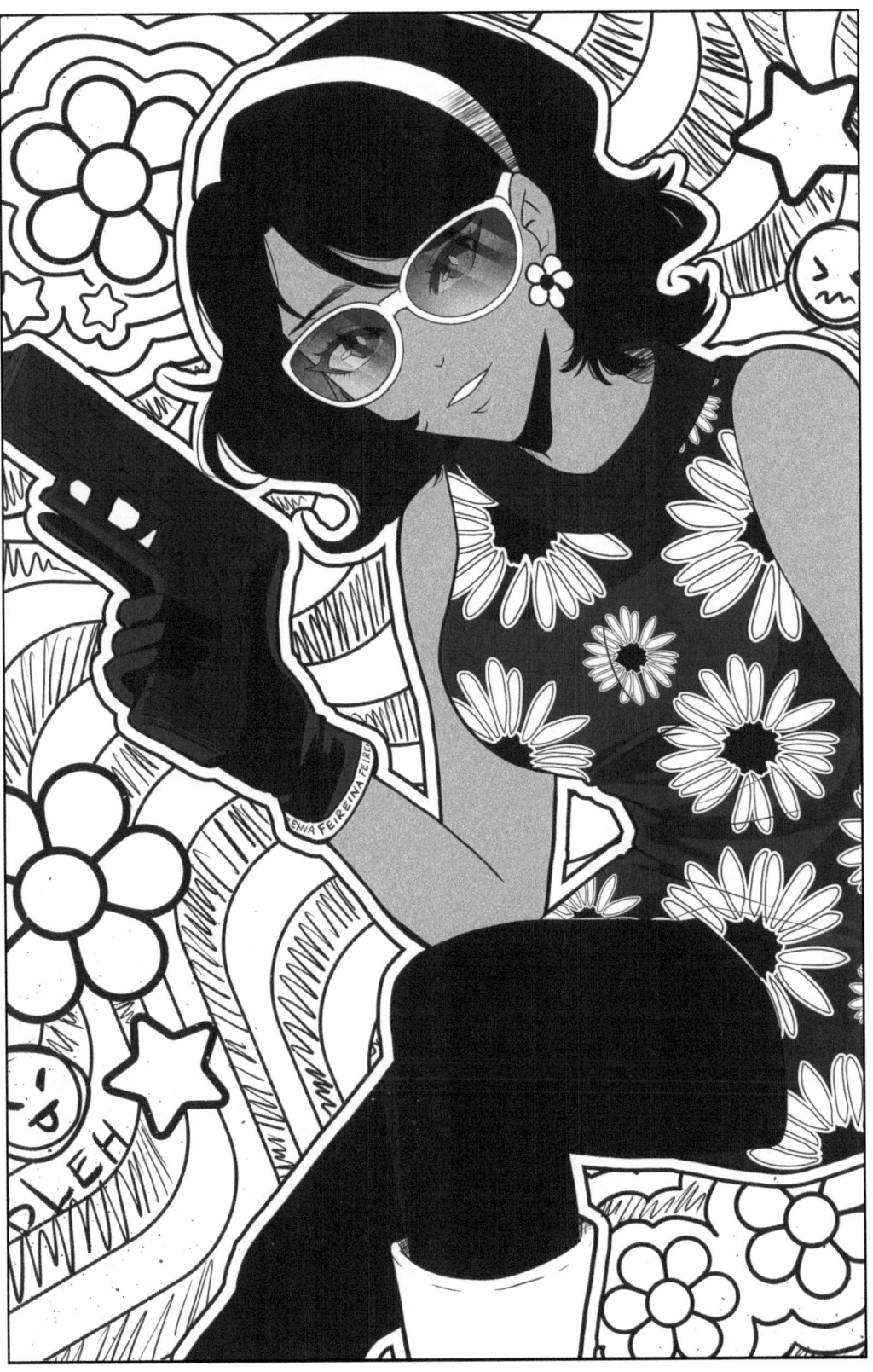

My neck hurts

This is a posture check! Please straigthen your back, you don't want to turn into a shrimp.

I was hunched over for a long time while I worked on this piece because I decided to add a lot of small details into the illustration. If Rorie was the one that decided to set the style for the collection, then Azrael (this character) was the one who cemented it.

Azrael, Rorie, Noah and Nomusa are characters from my story "Dreaming of Aurora". He's in love with Noah but he doesn't know it yet. This is why they both have dolls of each other! I wanted to add that as a cute little detail.

I used the wingdings font for the signs on his shoulder and let me be honest and say that I forgot what it said. Sorry.

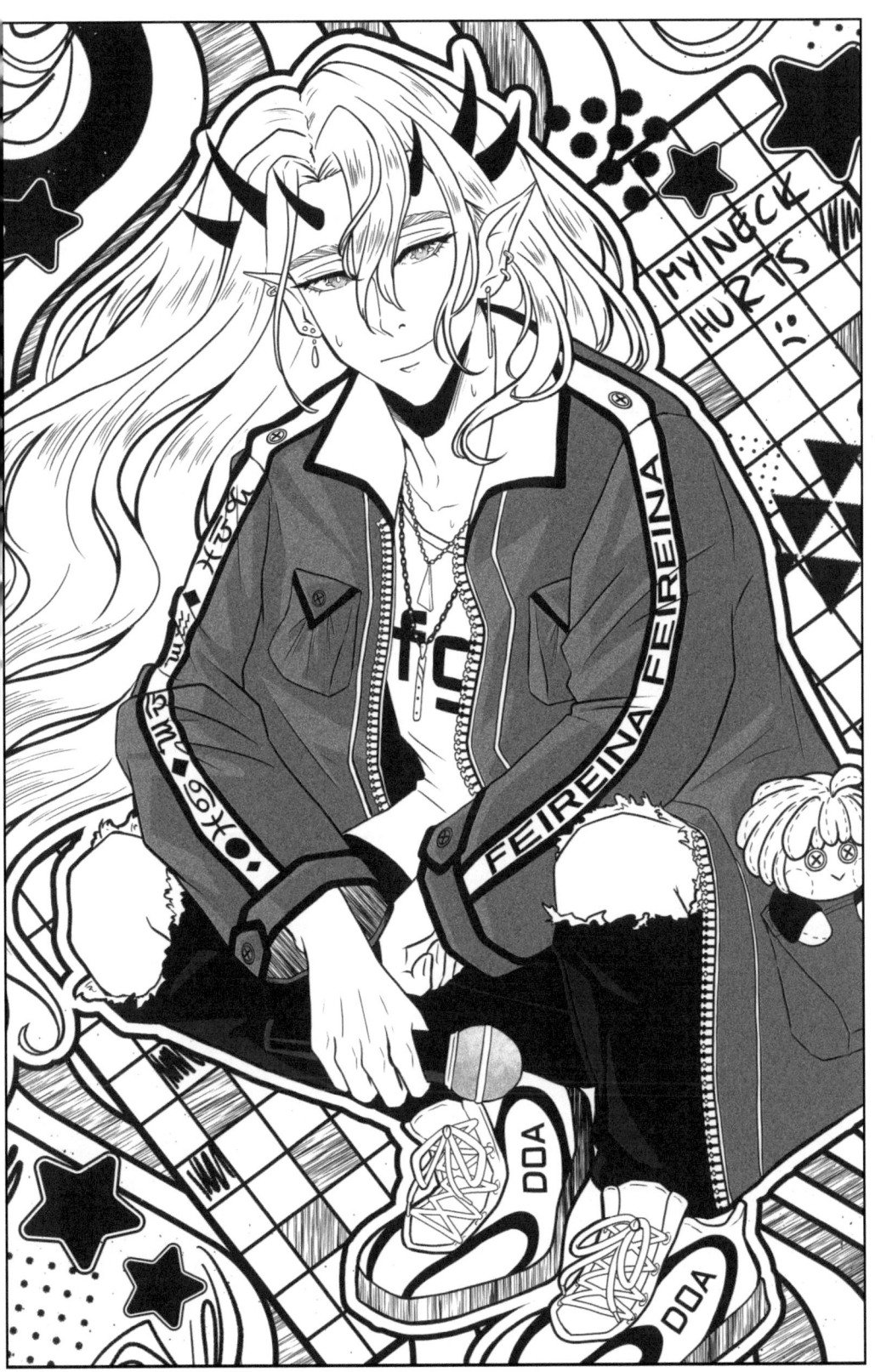

No thoughts head empty

This is definitely one of my favourite illustrations that came out of inktober. And no, it's not because she's part of my avatar. I based my avatar off three characters of this book. You will meet the other two soon!

This character here I still have to give a name.

I really love her bunny headphones in this illustration!
It was a bit difficult to draw and I was really frustrated while I was drawing it on stream, but in the end I think it turned out great!

Shameless plug, but check out my twitch channel at twitch.tv/feireina

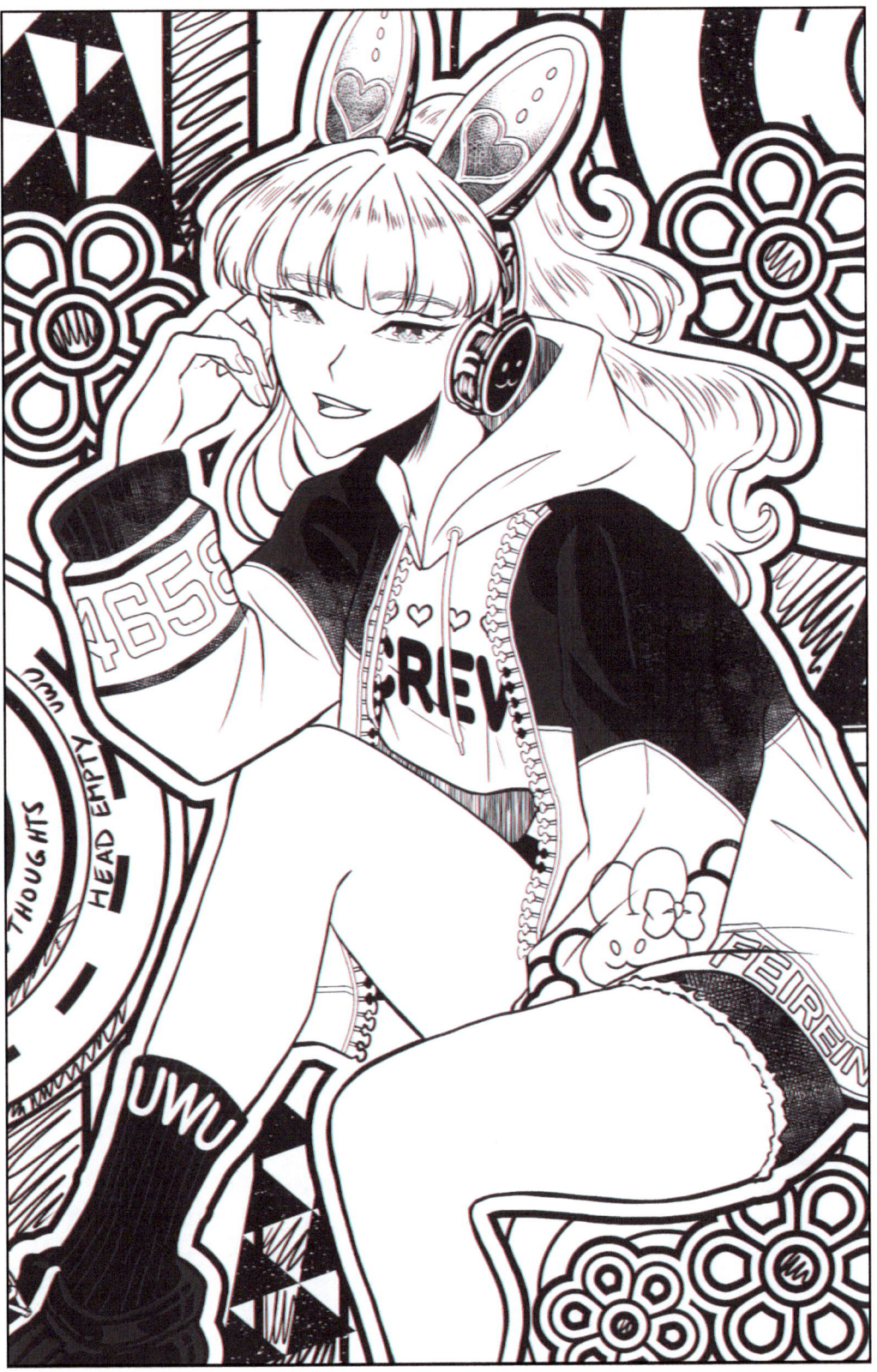

I took a nap and woke up at midnight

This here is another one of my avatars! I got my pigtails from her.

I'm actually planning to put her in my story "Dreaming of Aurora" as a side character with a tragic past.

I'm so excited to write more about her, but that might take a while for me to get to as she also hasn't got a name yet. I'm thinking of making a poll in my discord server for people to vote on once the time comes to properly introduce her to the story.

You might have noticed this already, but every piece has a tiny little note I wrote on the sides which happens to be the titles for the pages. For this one here it's "I TOOK A NAP AND WOKE UP AT MIDNIGHT QAQ".

For those wondering what "QAQ" means... it's just a cute crying emote.

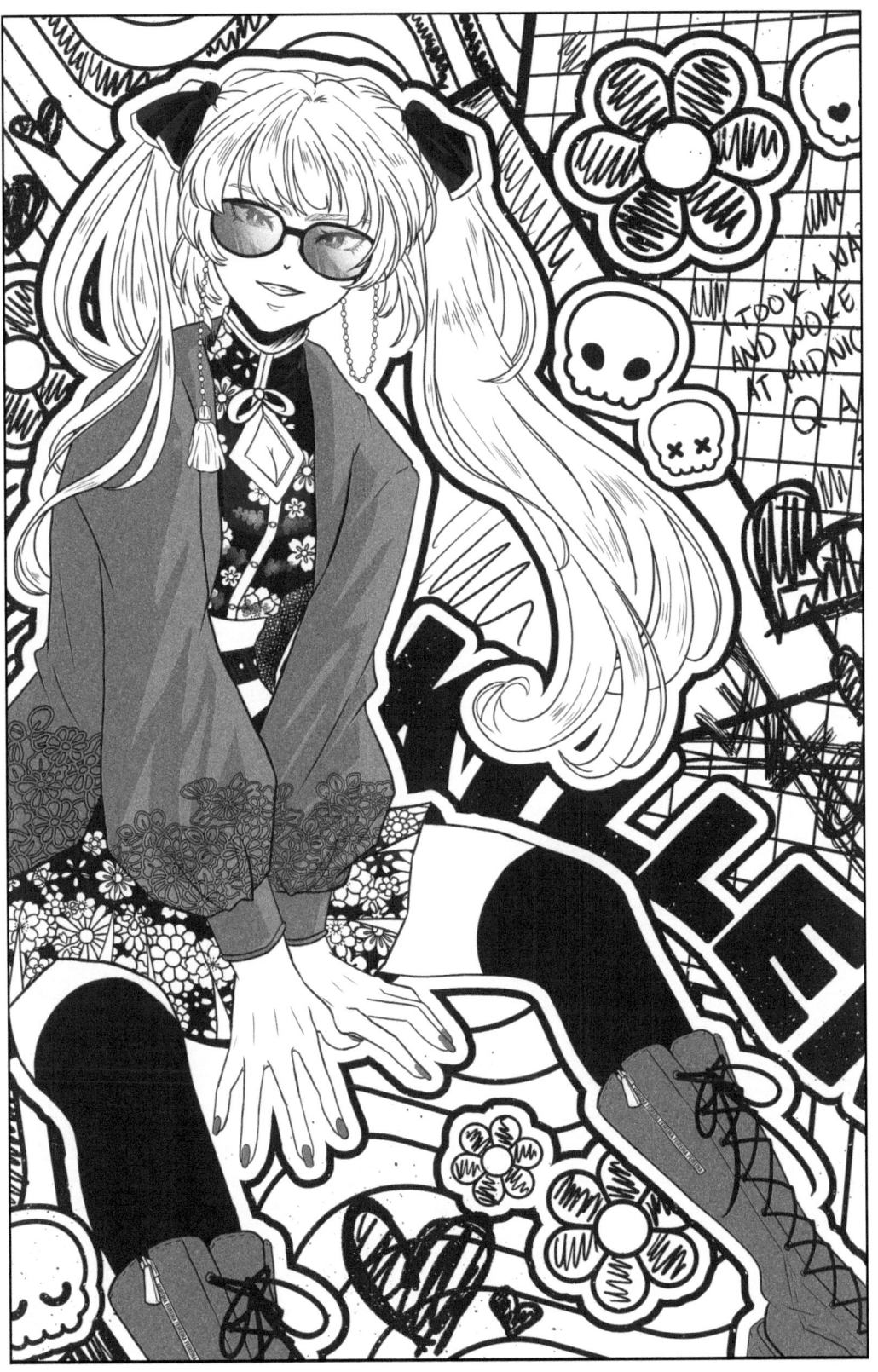

No space

The final character that I took traits from to create my twitch pngtuber! She actually has aqua coloured hair and my avatar got those traits from her. Same with the curly hair and the heart mole!

This character has a name unlike the other two. She's called Mari and she has a little sheep companion I forgot to draw called Sol.

And together they're Marisol!

I'm not gonna lie, but I was rushing this piece a lot because I went out with my family to visit a pumpkin farm. I found out that there are so many varieties of pumpkins. Some are even shaped like mushrooms??? And a lot of them are not edible.

Also, I only really wanted to go because I wanted to have some pumpkin soup. I got it at a buffet and it was really mid.

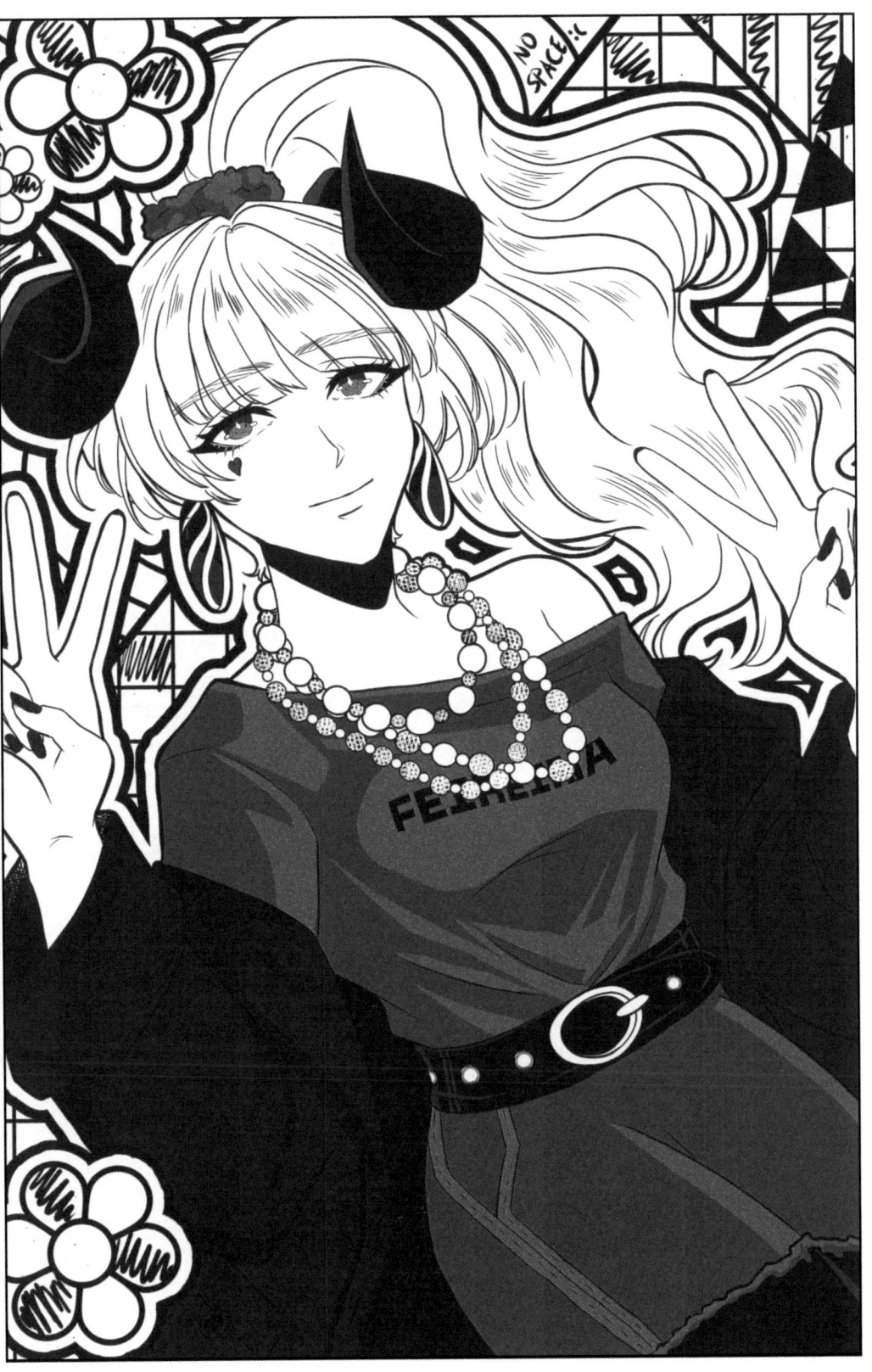

I forgot to write something

We're finally introducing my friends' characters in this page! This deadly lady belongs to Goldenpeel and her name is Grace!

I actually know a little bit about her. I once asked Gold what crime she would commit if she was in a wanted poster, and he replied with "Arson, assault, murder. Anything physical." She's also something like a vigilante! That's very punk if you ask me.

Also drawing the spikes on her shoulder was because of a memory I had of a schoolmate of mine in art school.

She always wore this leather jacket with spikes on her shoulders and the spikes were exactly at my eye level. I always worried that it will one day poke my eye out whenever we're crammed together in the tram on the way to school.

Luckily nothing like that happened. I miss her and the weird pendant she filled with her blood.

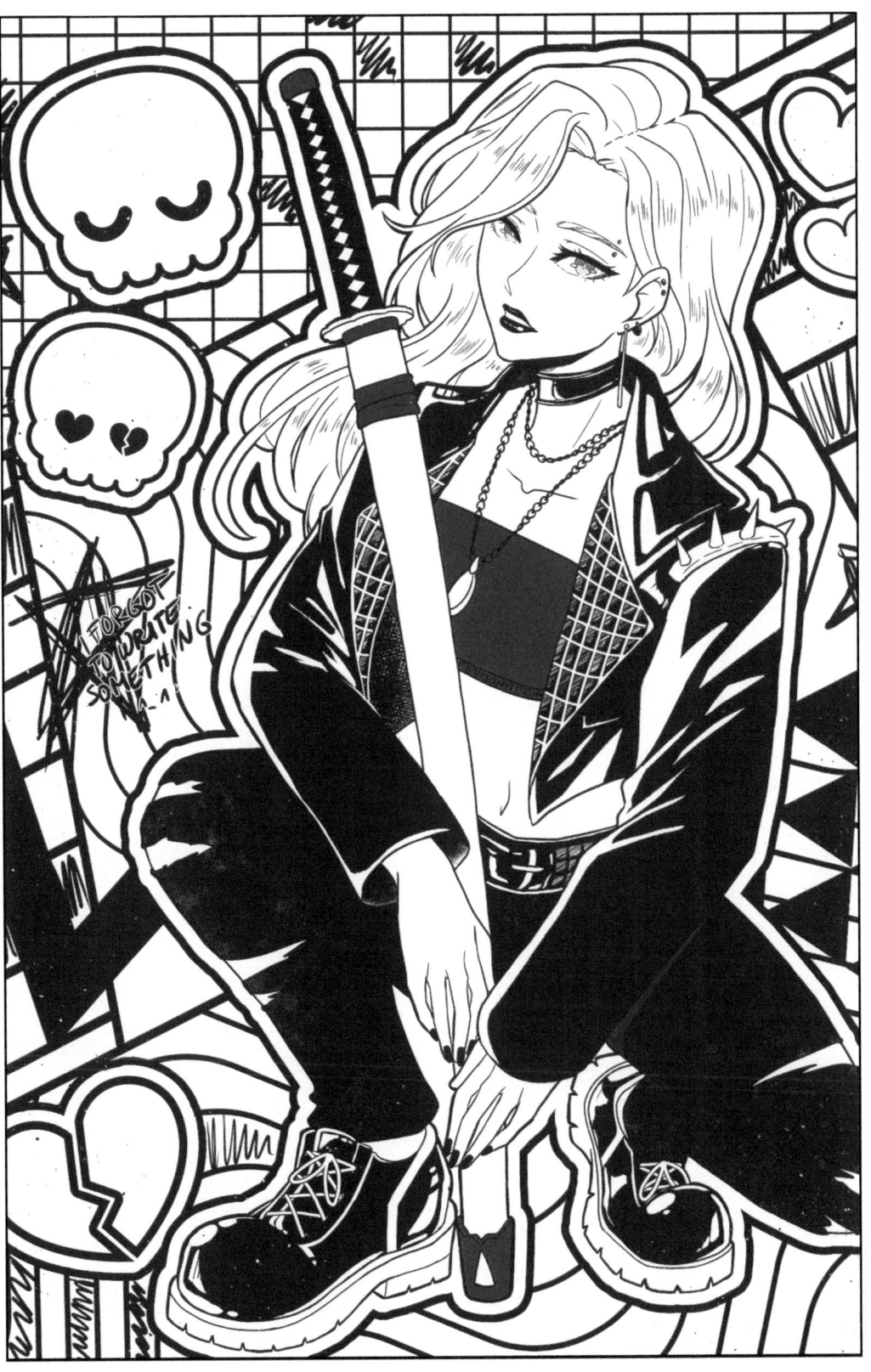

Why am I always tired?

At this point I'm already a day late because of my visit to the pumpkin farm. Still, I had a lot of fun drawing this!

It's definitely one of my favourite illustrations. She's so cool and naughty! I love drawing characters who are a bit on the bratty side.

I had trouble trying to figure out what to do with that jacket she's wearing. I was wondering what kind of pattern I should use. In the end I decided to just use the same flower pattern from the background and hey, it worked!

Work smarter, not harder as they say.

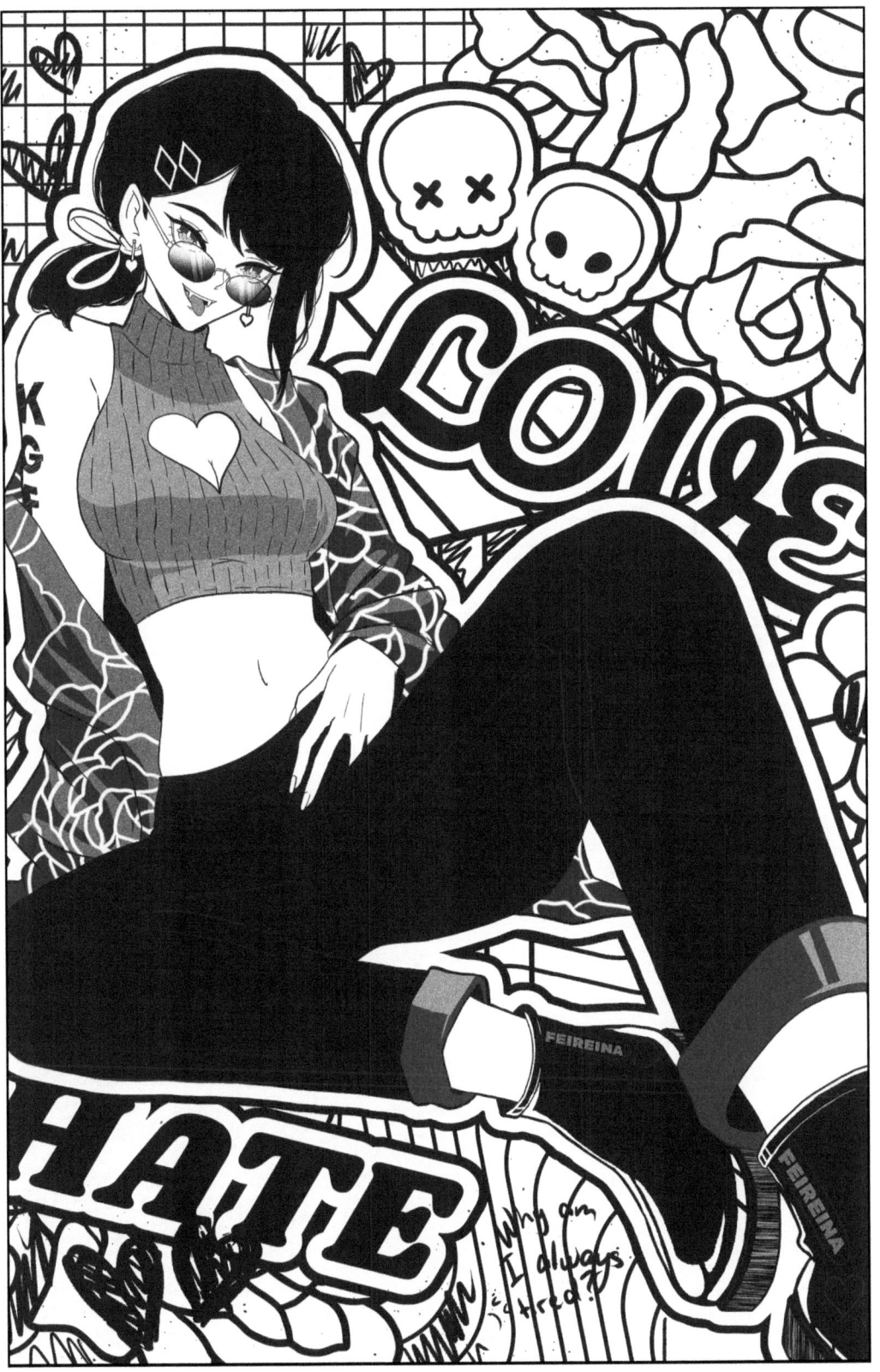

I'm still trying to catch up

Look at those fangs! Would you let her bite you?

This outfit is so elegant and cozy. If you took out the cardigan and replaced it with a blazer, she could totally be working as a banker. Not only will she suck your blood, she'll suck your finances too!

To be honest, she reminds me a little bit of my little sister and the outfits she wears for work. She sells insurance, so she tend to go for the more elegant clothes, but I don't think her job will allow her to meet clients wearing this kind of cardigan even though its super cute.

As always, corporate takes out all the fun in things.

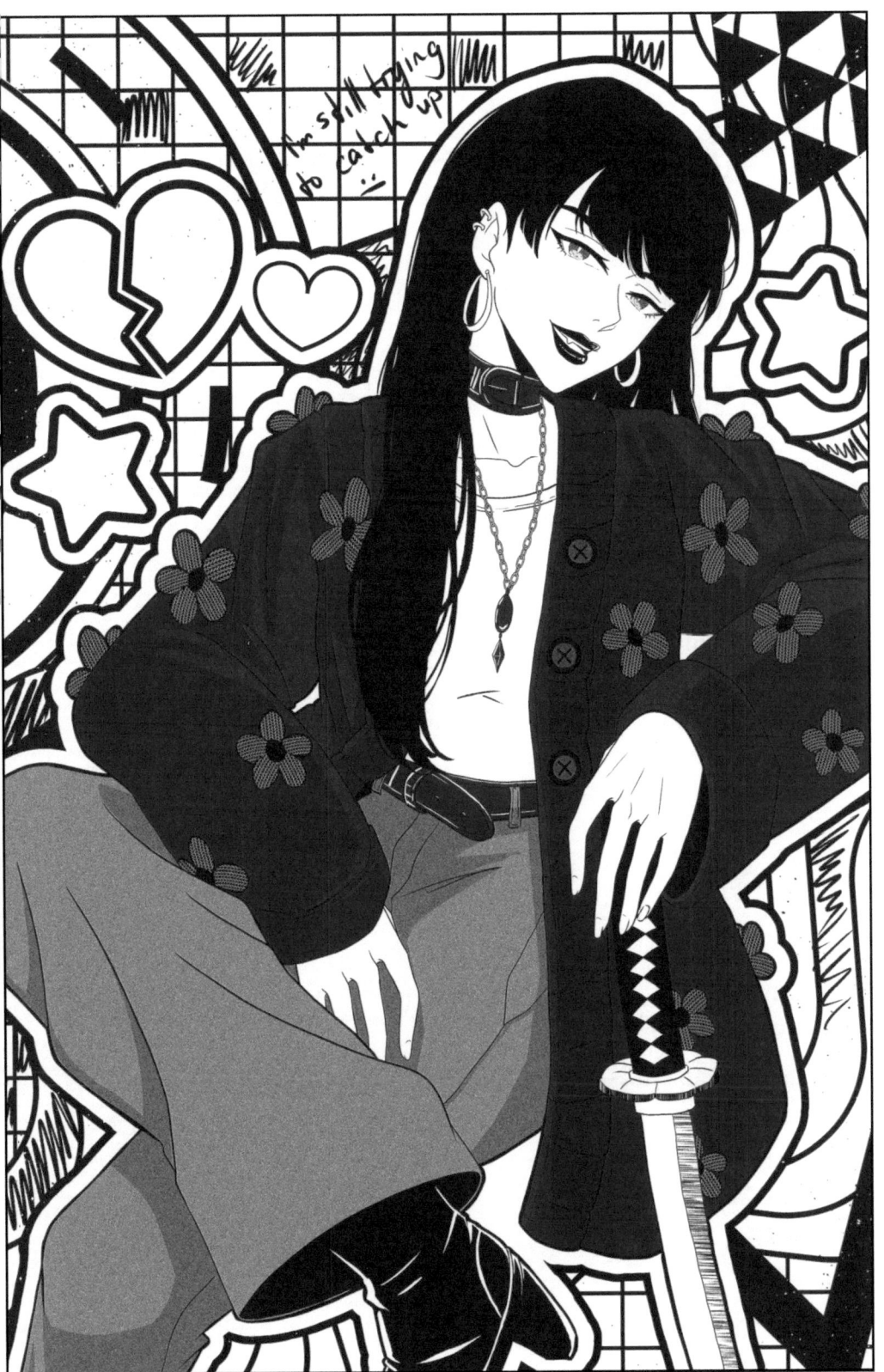

Shut up and talk - Fei

There's a small story behind my little scribbled note. I was actually drawing this live on stream, but I was so tired my brain was not braining anymore. So I said "Shut up and talk" to myself while streaming and it took me a moment to realise that it made no sense.

This is why you shouldn't stream when half asleep.
You start spewing nonsense.

Aside from that, this is the thinnest lineart I've ever drawn! I'm actually super proud of it since it's something I've never been able to do before.

Art Tipp:
Depending on your coloring style, thin lineart might not be ideal to have! If you have a more painterly style, it would definitely benefit you to have thing lineart, but if you prefer to keep your colours flat with little shading, then a thicker lineart would look best because it will help your character standout and add more dimension to your piece!

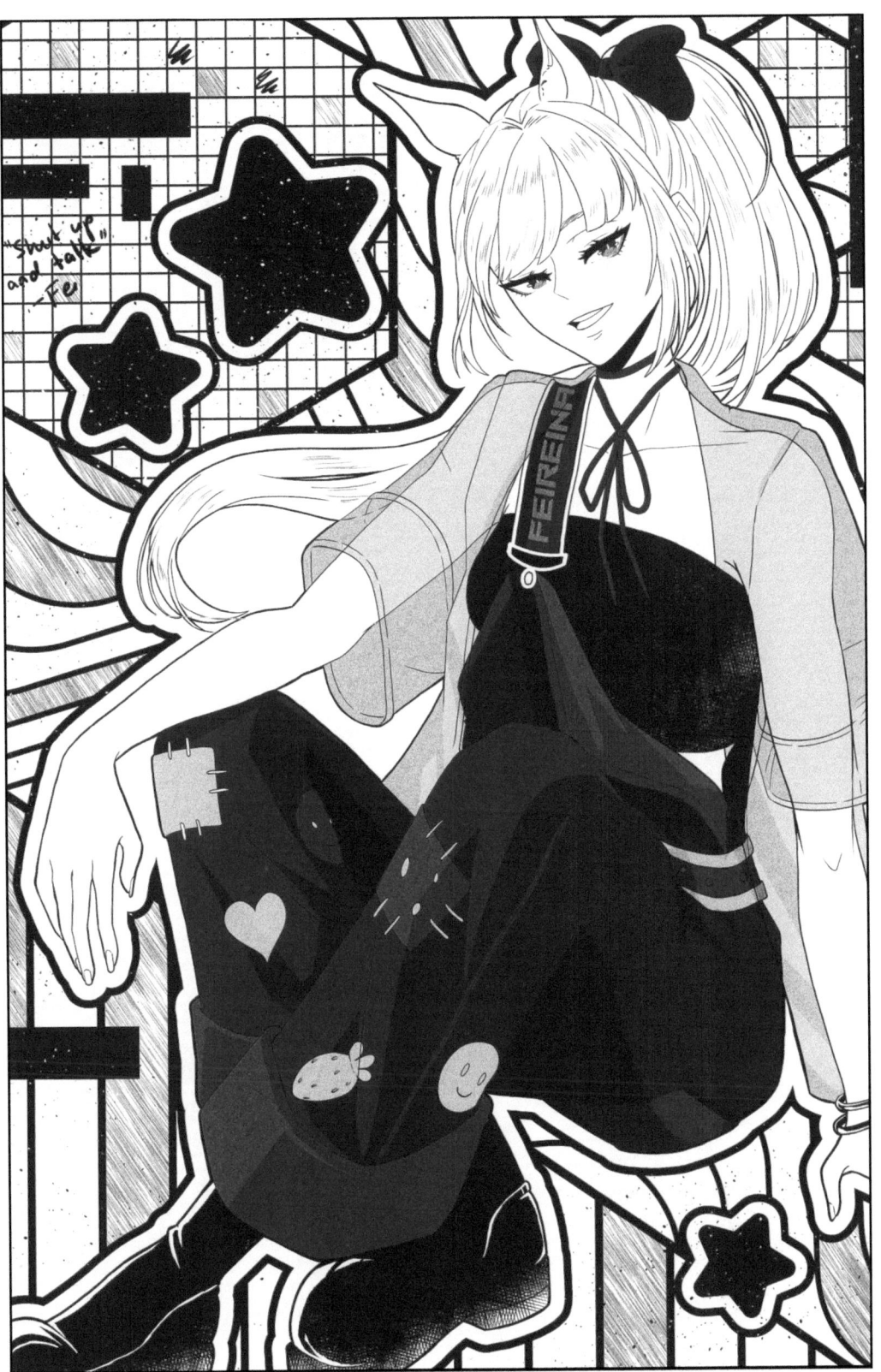

Hellow :3

Sweet summer child you are so cute! She's probably one of the more cuter characters I've drawn! She looks so cozy and ready to dance in the roaring 20s! But don't be fooled by her cuteness! She's part of the Killer GF! She'll probably poison your martini.

Moon, the owner of this character, mentioned Nxde, a song by a kpop group called G-Idle when I showed it to her. And honestly I didn't even know they had a song that uses the roaring 20s aesthetics until then, but it was good to know because I really enjoy their songs!

Oh, in case you're wondering, your eyes are not fooling you and it's not an error on my part. This character does have two different shades of eye colours!

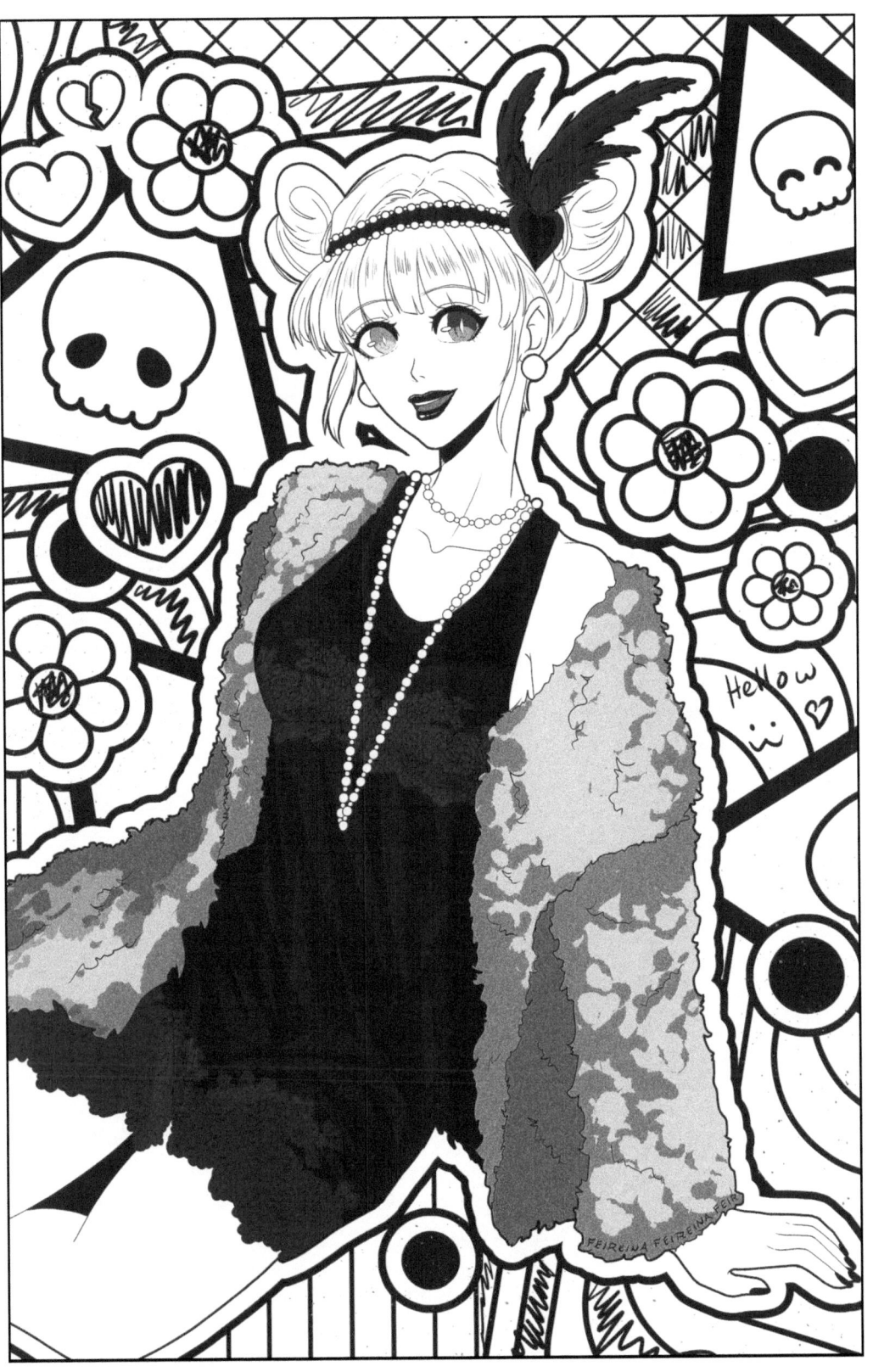

Don't smoke kids

It's been a while since I've drawn a guy, yes? This is Robek's avatar! He's infamous for his bright red hair, but I obviously couldn't add colour in. So I thought I'd add in things that Robek likes and is associated with.

I added the fishes and fishing rod because he sometimes tweet that he's "gone fishing".

I used to think that he meant it literally, but apparently it was code for him that he's taking some days off social media? I don't even know if Robek has ever gone fishing in real life.

That aside, Robek really loves his memes and Nic Cage and Ryan Gosling. So I thought, why not add them in?

If possible it's always good to add Nic Cage anywhere and everywhere. And Ryan Gosling is a beautiful man, he was great in the Barbie movie so in he goes!

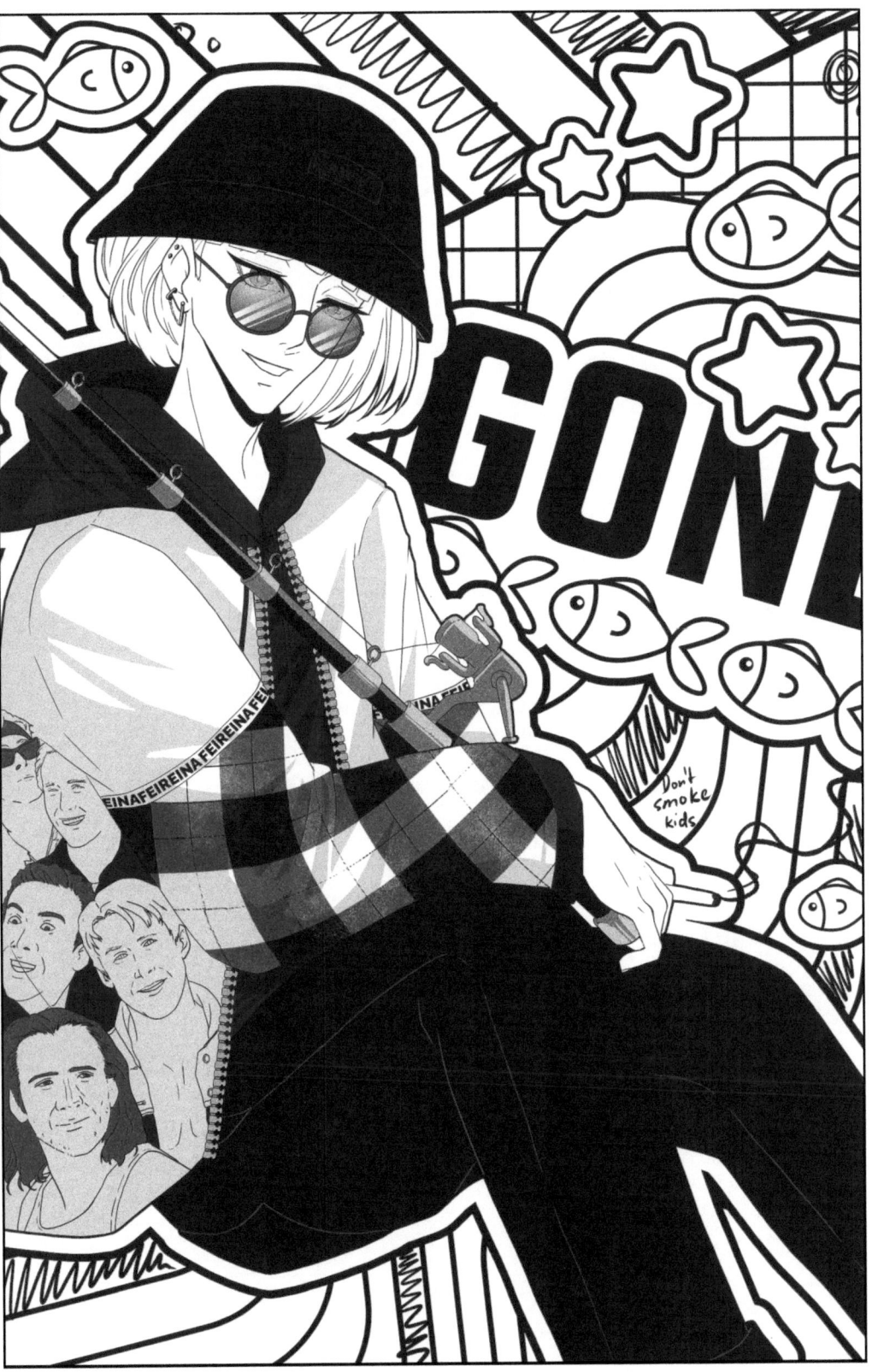

My sleep schedule is fcked -.- zzz

Here is the lovely salary lady Miyako-chan modeling for me! She's sai7's OC and she's just adorable!

I was having a bit of trouble with her pose, because for some reason, I initially drew her shoulders too broad. It seems I have forgotten how to draw a female character for a short time, hence why I was struggling with the pose.

I think that around this time I started realising how much faster I got with the lineart now that my art process has been perfected like a well oiled machine.

Still, I'm two days late with inktober already because I joined a family dinner at my little sisters' new apartment. But it was worth it because the veggie lasagna was bomb.

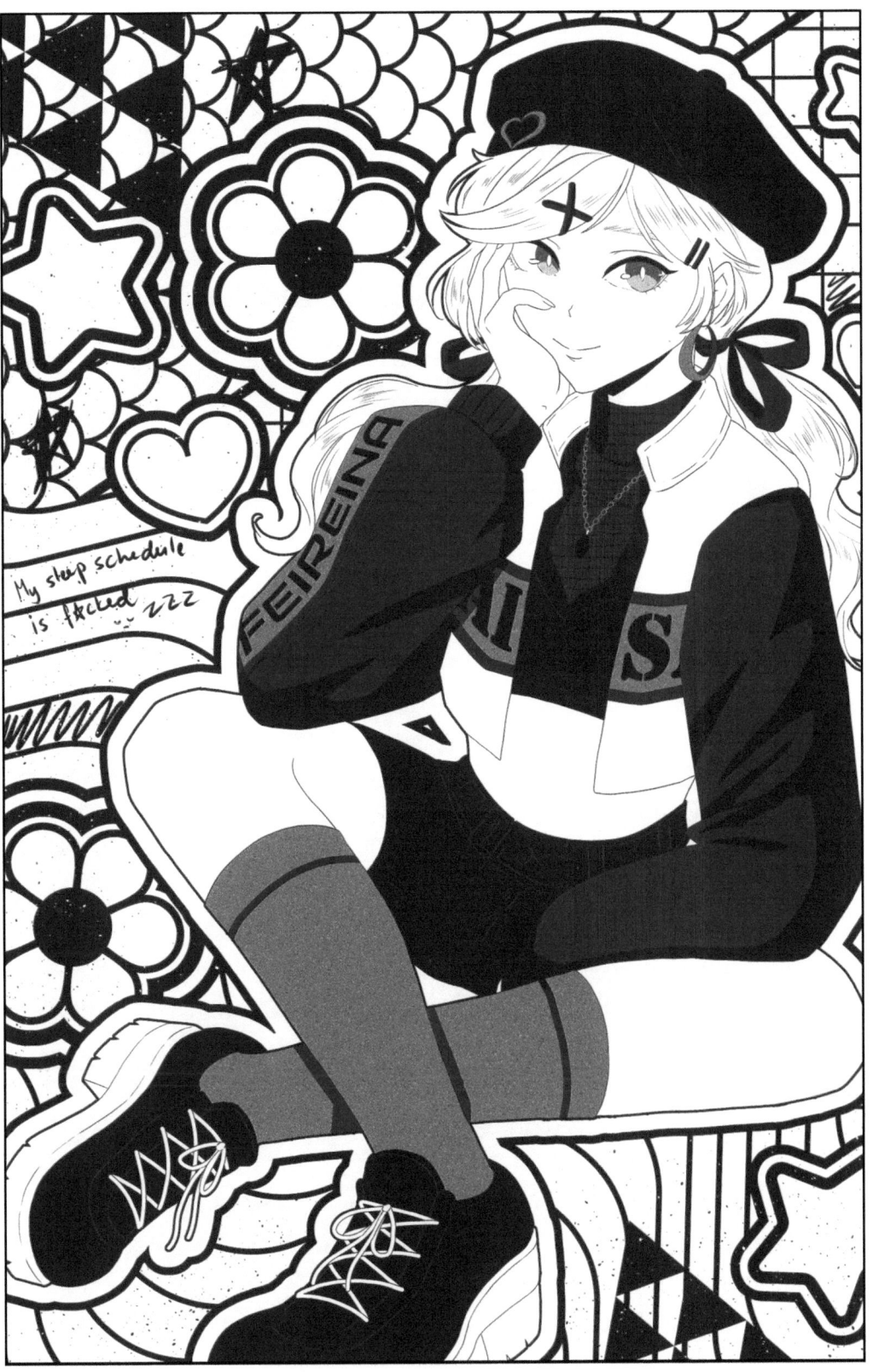

I'm wide awake at 1am :D Yay sugar rush!!!

I remember finishing Vanarics' OC in the middle of the night, it was at around 3 am or something because I wrote a note on the illustration that "I'm wide awake at 1am :D" while working on it.

This is the start of my new sleep cycle. I used to wake up like a normal person at around 8am, but because I had a bout of insomnia, my sleep schedule became messed up. Currently I'm writing this at around 1am too, when I should be asleep.

Anyways, while I was drawing this, I kept thinking "How can I make this illustration look cooler?"

The answer is accessories!

Adding a scarf or sunglasses to any character makes them instantly cooler and more stylish. I think that's also the case for real life too!

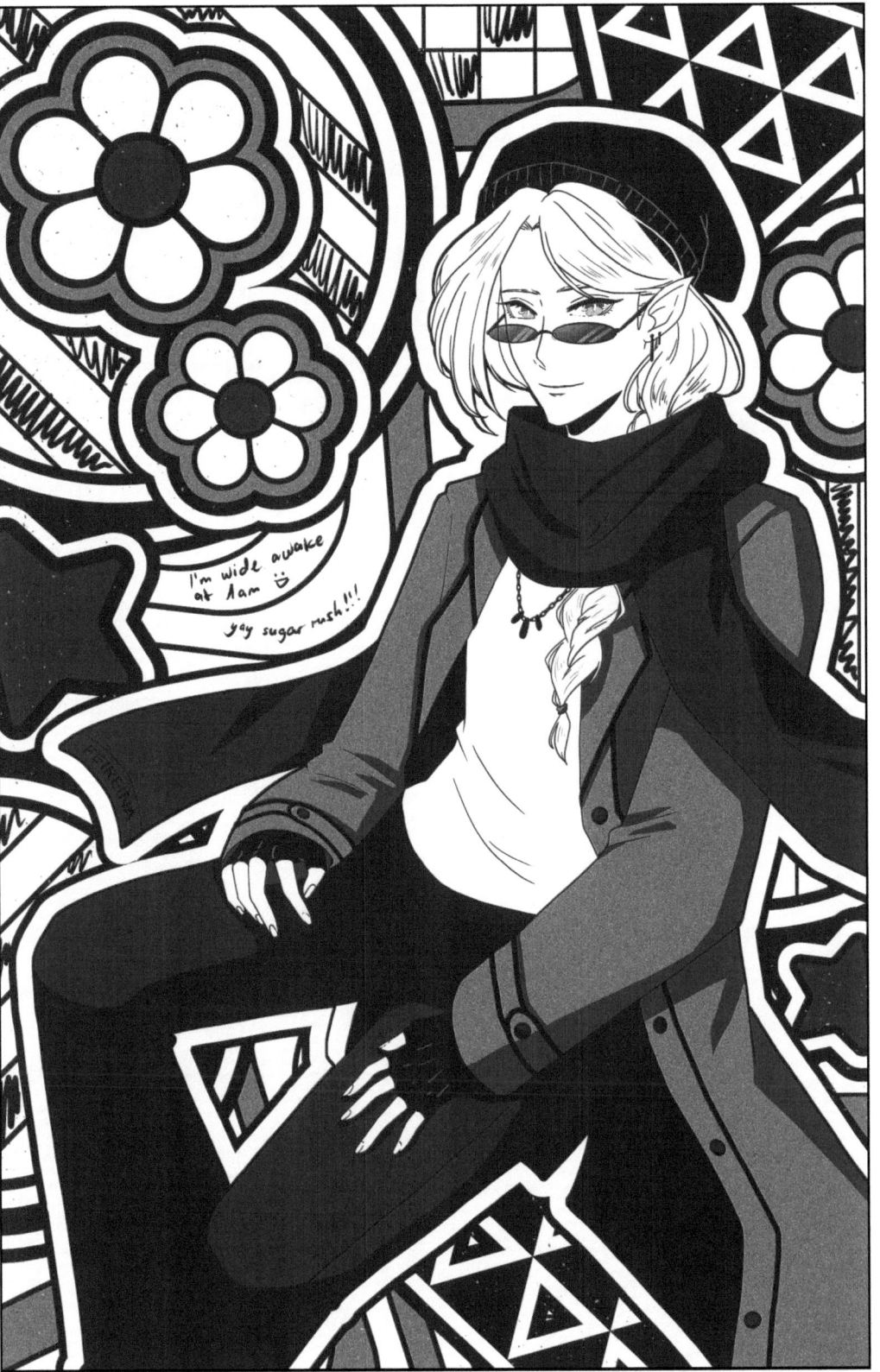

I had issues with my graphic card

One of my favourite illustrations! Honestly this surprised me when I finished it. I think I've improved so much since I started inktober! Good job me!

This illustration actually took pretty long to finish because of all the small accesories I gave her. But surprisingly enough, the hands were easy to draw. Sometimes it just seems like some art spirit posessed me to be able to draw hands so well without taking an hour off my life.

Oh yes, I also had issues with my graphic card while I was drawing this. It took me an hour to fix the problem.

It was so annoying.

I was on the verge of just going to sleep and letting future me deal with the problem. It was also a reminder that I need a new computer.

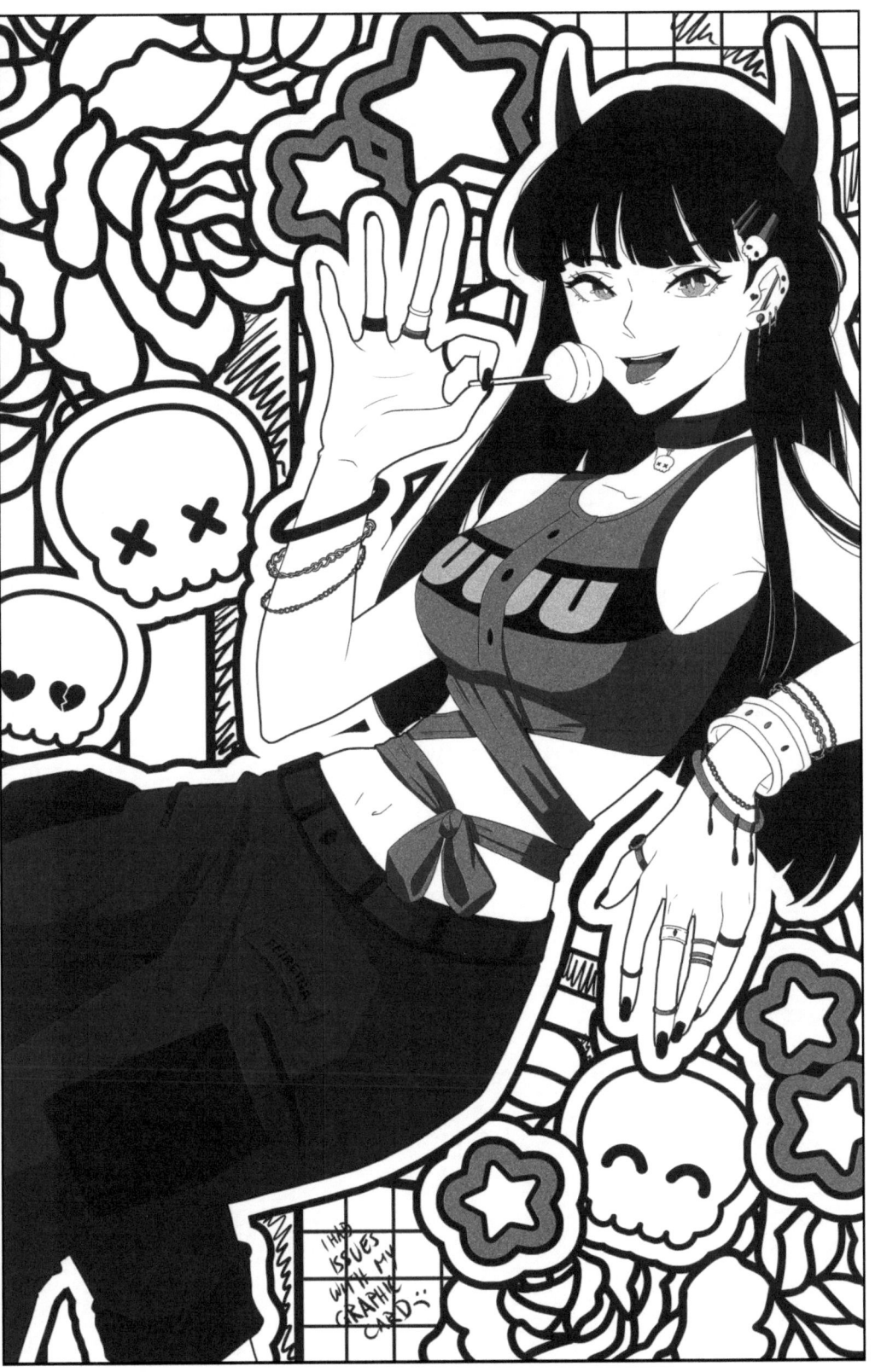

Nihonjin desu (leg)

Another husbando! This one here is actually based on the fact that this character was in a vault by an account called "oikawabest". So I thought I'd pay a tribute to that!

The most obvious part are the volleyballs. The more subtle hint is the number 13. It's actually Oikawas number when he was playing for Argentina!

Honestly, this outfit was pretty boring at the beginning and I was wondering what type of accessory he can have to make him look cooler. So while I was scrolling through pinterest and listening to music, the song MIC Drop by BTS came on. And I'm like "Wait a second, their outfits there are hella drippy". So I gave him a bandana because Yoongi was wearing one and BOOM. Instant drip.

On another note, the little scribbled text is a bit of an inside joke. I'm not actually japanese, but there's a pun with nihonjin and legs over there.

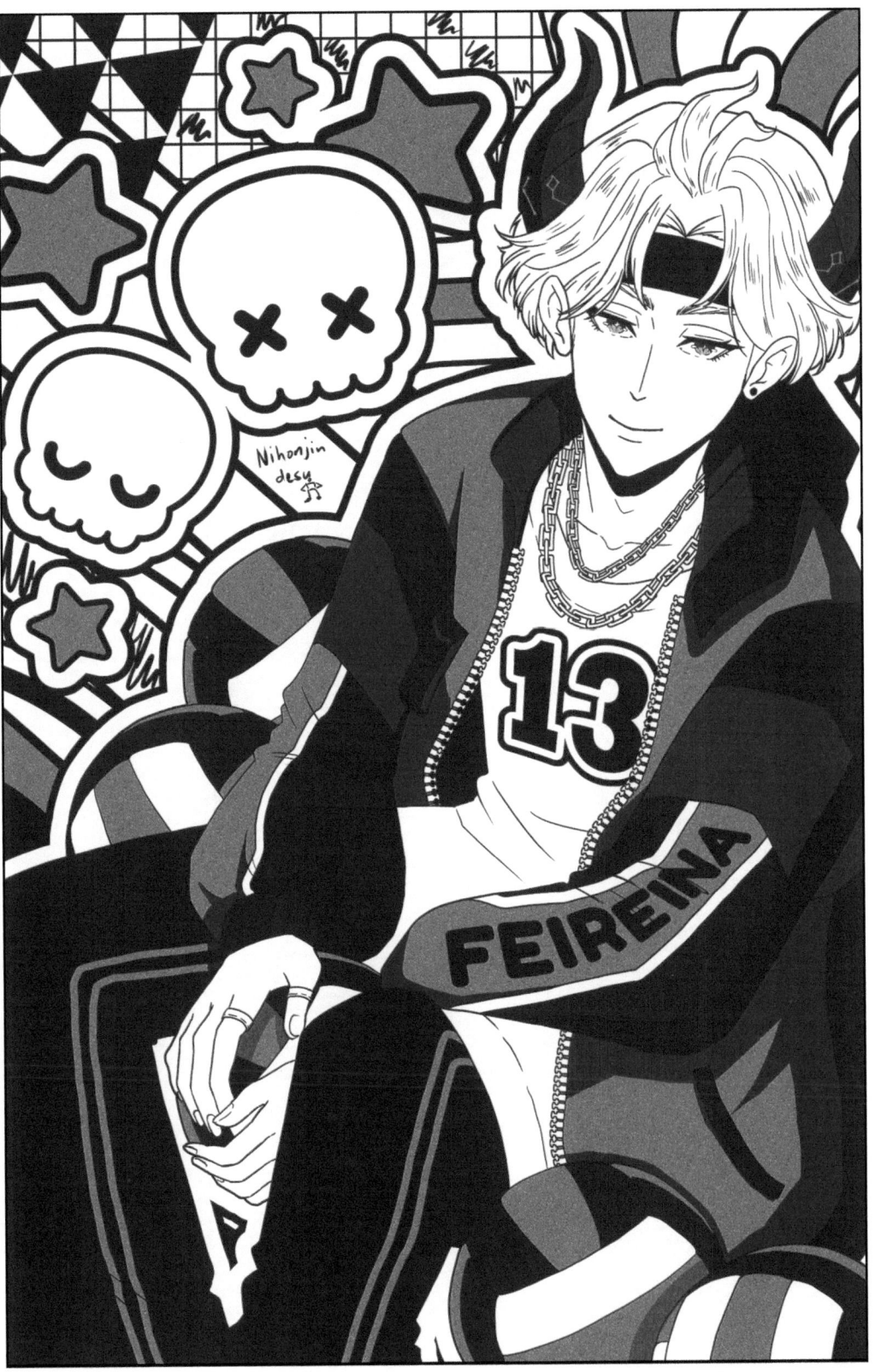

Late again >:(

And one more dude! I'm not gonna lie, drawing this was difficult because I wasn't sure about the pose or the outfit. But what I did know is that I needed him to have his katana.

I was originally going to use the rose pattern that I have for his coat, but I thought that it made no sense to use that. After looking at all the artworks datdegenboi commissioned of this character, it was obvious that he was associated with water.

That's why I added water elements to his coat and added the fishes around him because they're cute.

Art Tipp:

Most art program has a feature that enables you to create straight lines easily.

For Clip Studio and Photoshop, it's the polyline tool.

For Procreate, you can drag a line and hold your pen down until it turns straight (or turns into a circle depending on the shape.)

And yes, I'm telling you this because I forgot polyline tools existed.

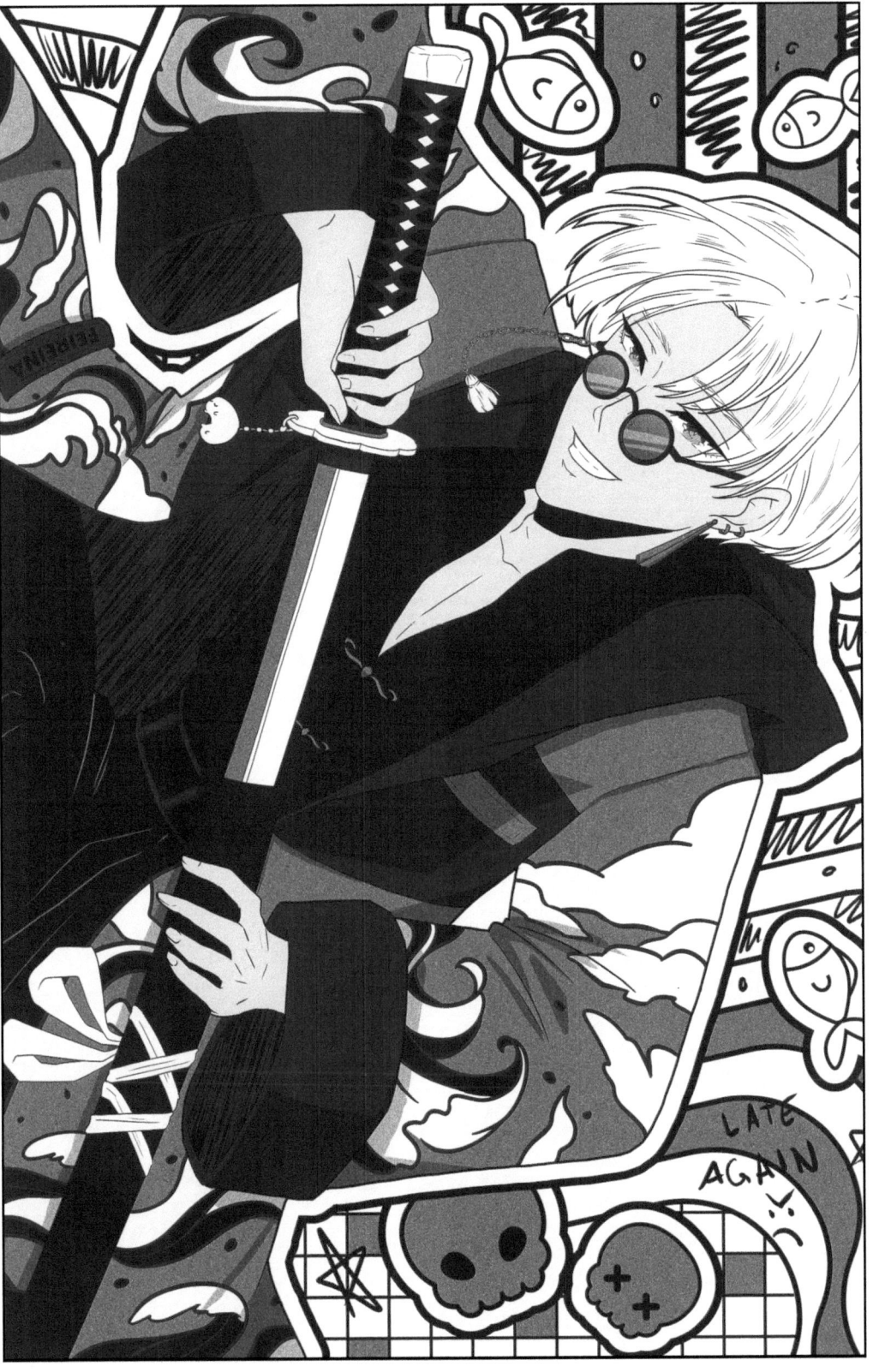

Art spirit possessed me

This piece is probably one of the best pieces in the collection. It's definitely in the top 5 for me! I'm not sure why, but I really went ham on the details for this one.

I actually have a prompt of clothes or accessories that I focus on in the inktober pieces, that I later on started ignoring because I wanted to draw hot ladies.

The prompt for this one was "nails". That's why her nails are very much the focus of the piece. She also is the only one in the whole collection that has nail art done! Most of the time the other illustrations only has their nails painted.

Also I'm not going to lie, but "Sk8er Boi" by Avril Lavigne was playing on my spotify when I was drawing this, that's why her vibes is giving a mix of "She was a sk8er gworl and she did ballet".

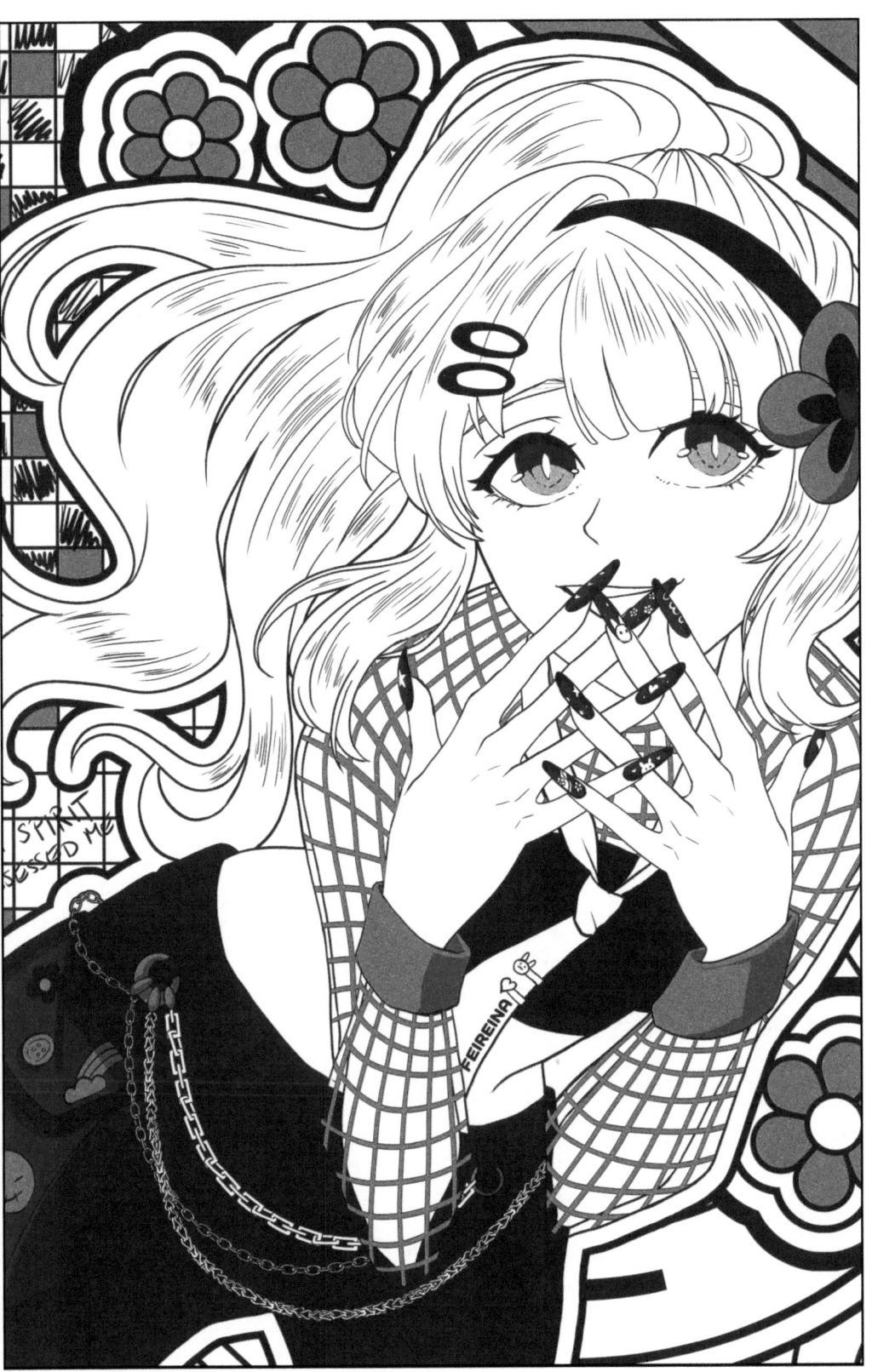

Say GMEOW

GMEOW! It means good morning in cat.

This was really easy for me to draw and I had so much fun with the pose!

I originally wanted to give her tail a ribbon with a bell on it, kind of like in the anime "Tokyo Mew Mew". But in the end I decided against it because composition wise, it did not look good, especially because I wanted to add the "GMEOW" text behind her.

However, I still wanted to give her some sort of bell accessory. That's when it occured to me that I can have the bells in her hair, because her hair is taking up a lot of the composition too, so I might as well try it out.
I really love the end result!

This is also the first time I added the cat elements in the backgrounds because I wanted something cute along with her too!

Art Tipp:

Always sketch out the background too! You can put the character and background sketches in seperate layers so you can experiment with compositions!

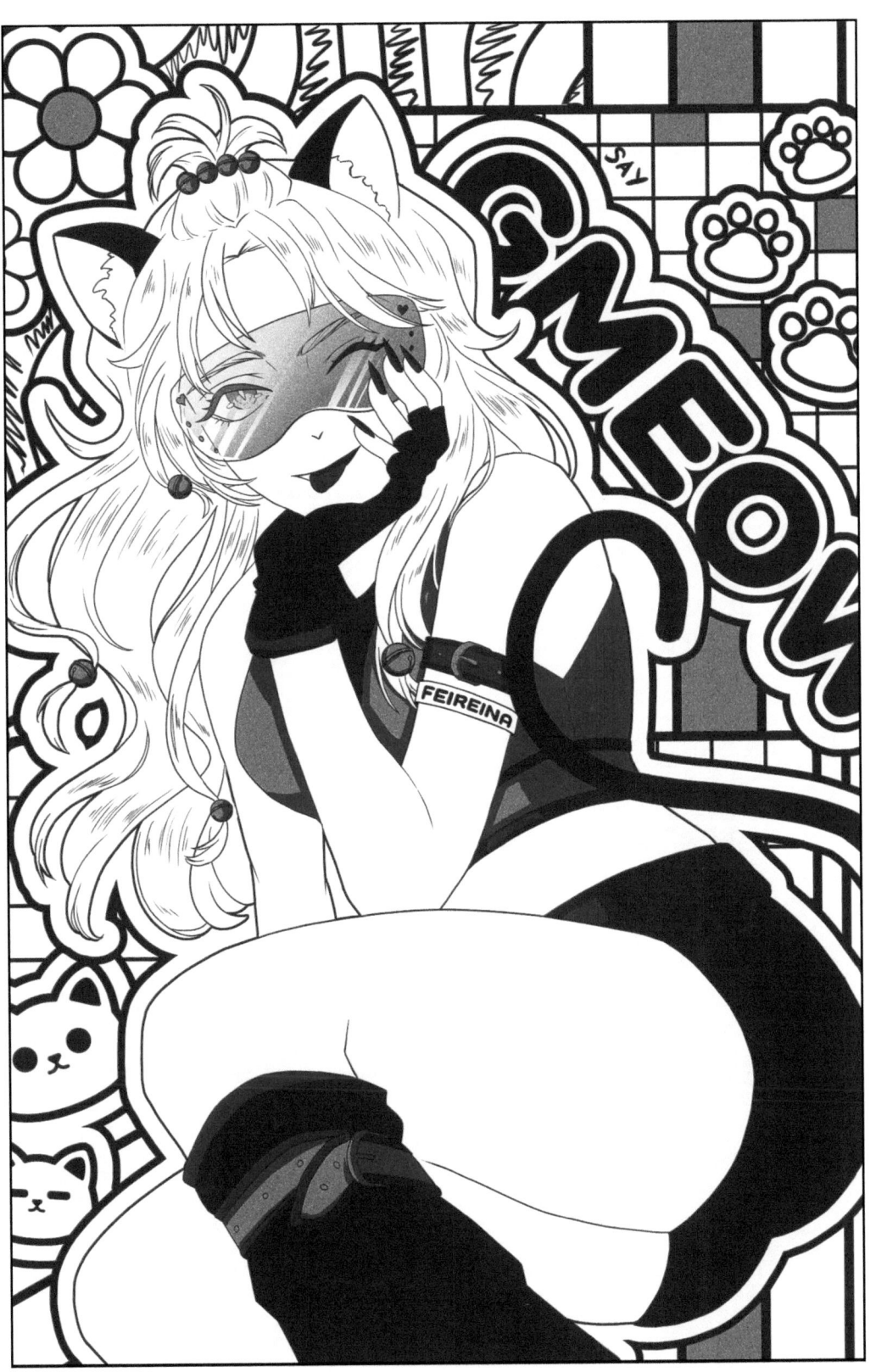

Live, laugh, love cat ladies

Deep down in my heart, I'm a cat lady, even if I own a cute clingy dog right now. If my dog wasn't so aggresive when it comes to cats, I might get myself a kitty. I always enjoyed watching cat and dog interactions on tiktok, they're just so cute! But as I mentioned before, my dog doesn't like them.

But enough about me! Let's talk about this piece! This one is for my friend Kazadi! The original reference picture of this character had her wearing a black turtleneck and I thought to myself "How can I yassify that?" and I just took out the turtle neck and made her wear a bra. But it has the stripe thing-y from the turtle neck... so technically that should still count right?

And because it's Kazadi, cats are a must! She runs a cat shelter in the Philippines and it would be great if you guys also checked out her twitter account to see how you can help her!

I also added the moon and stars earrings because she loves Sailor Moon.

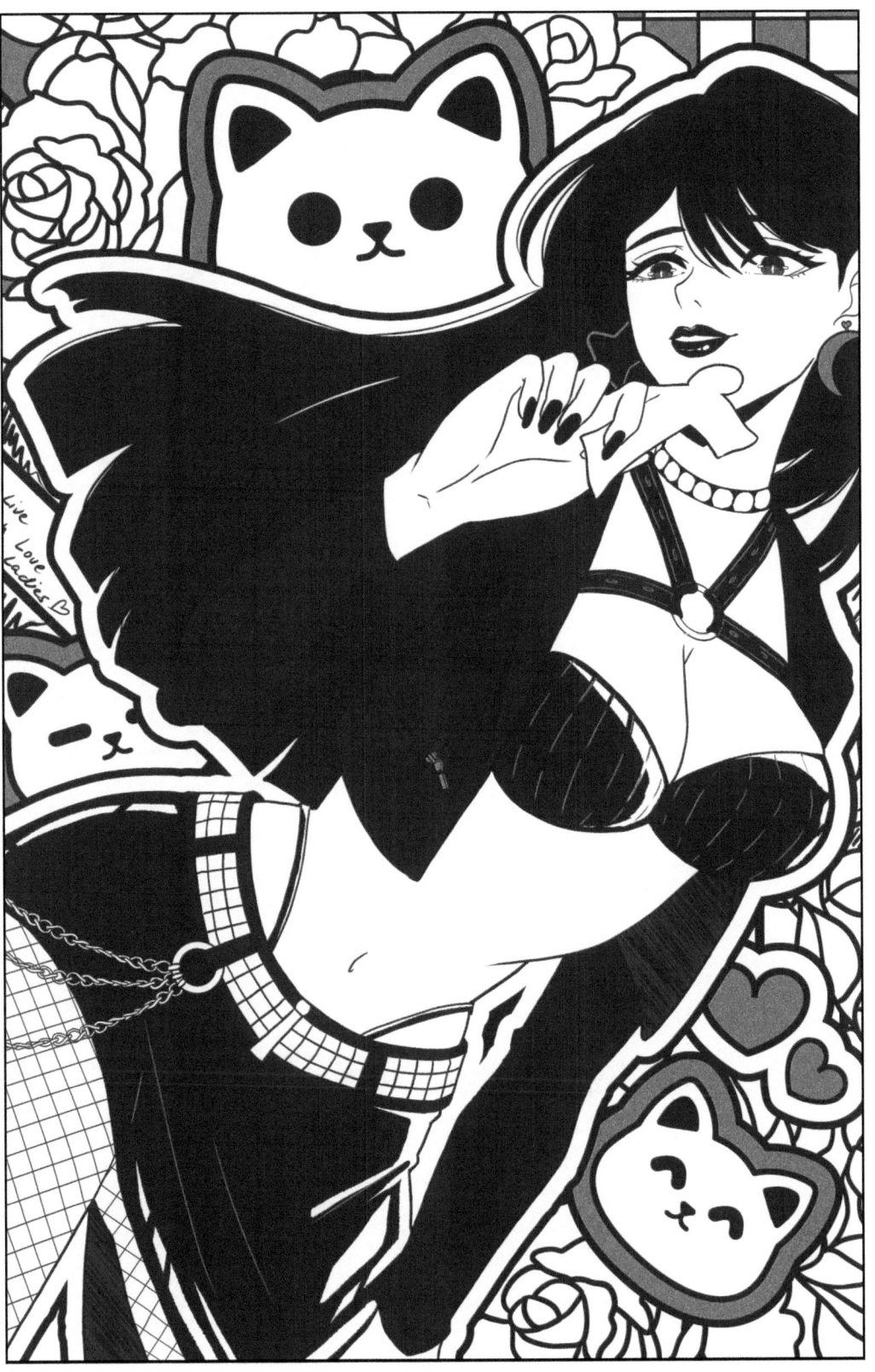

Autumn weather makes me so tired

Autumn is my favourite season. Just watching the trees turn orange is a sight to behold. Not to mention they're absolutely gorgeous to look at on a bright blue sky.

Which makes sense because they're complimentary colours.

But I really dislike the beginnings of autumn because it makes my skin so dry and makes me tired for no reason.

Because of that I honestly don't remember much when I was drawing this piece. Working on it was a huge blur. What I do remember was Shiomu messaging me back on the exact day I was working on this to say that I can use his character.

I had him on the list but didn't realise he hasn't given the ok until then. How lucky that he wrote to me on that day, otherwise things could have ended up awkward.

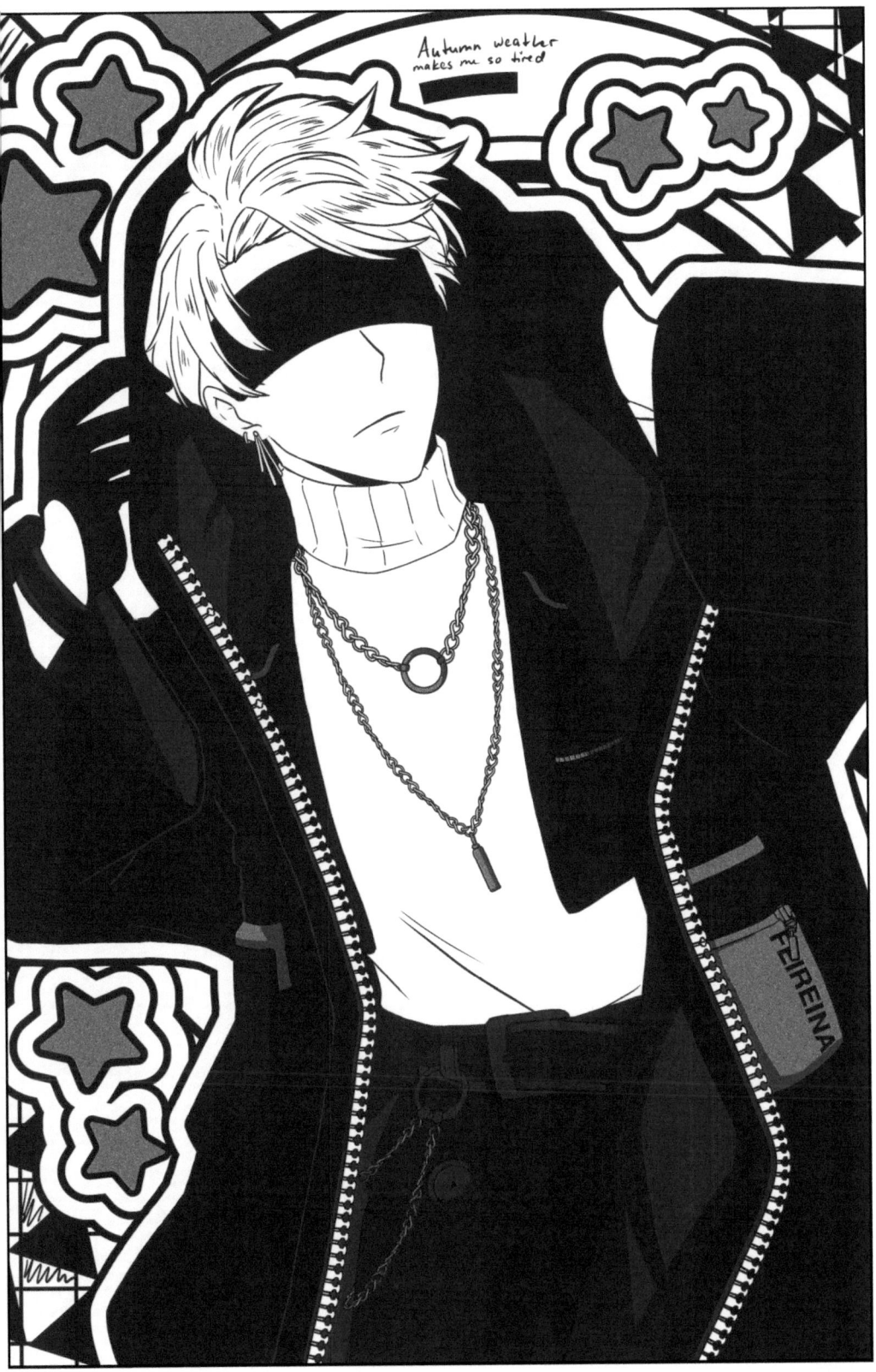

THICC THIGHS SAVE LIVES

Drawing this made me realise I really enjoy drawing thighs.

One special thing about this art is her belly piercing and where the chains lead to. I'm not saying what's going on, you can use your own imagination.

Art Tipp:

If you want to find a good sexy pose reference on pinterest, searching for "Hwasa, Nicki Minaj or E-girl" works really well.

Do note that if you do use this trick, your pinterest homepage might be sussy for a while. Also be careful when searching for more risque references on pinterest, they might ban you.

I already got a second warning from them and honestly I dont want to be banned just because I'm searching for some art references.

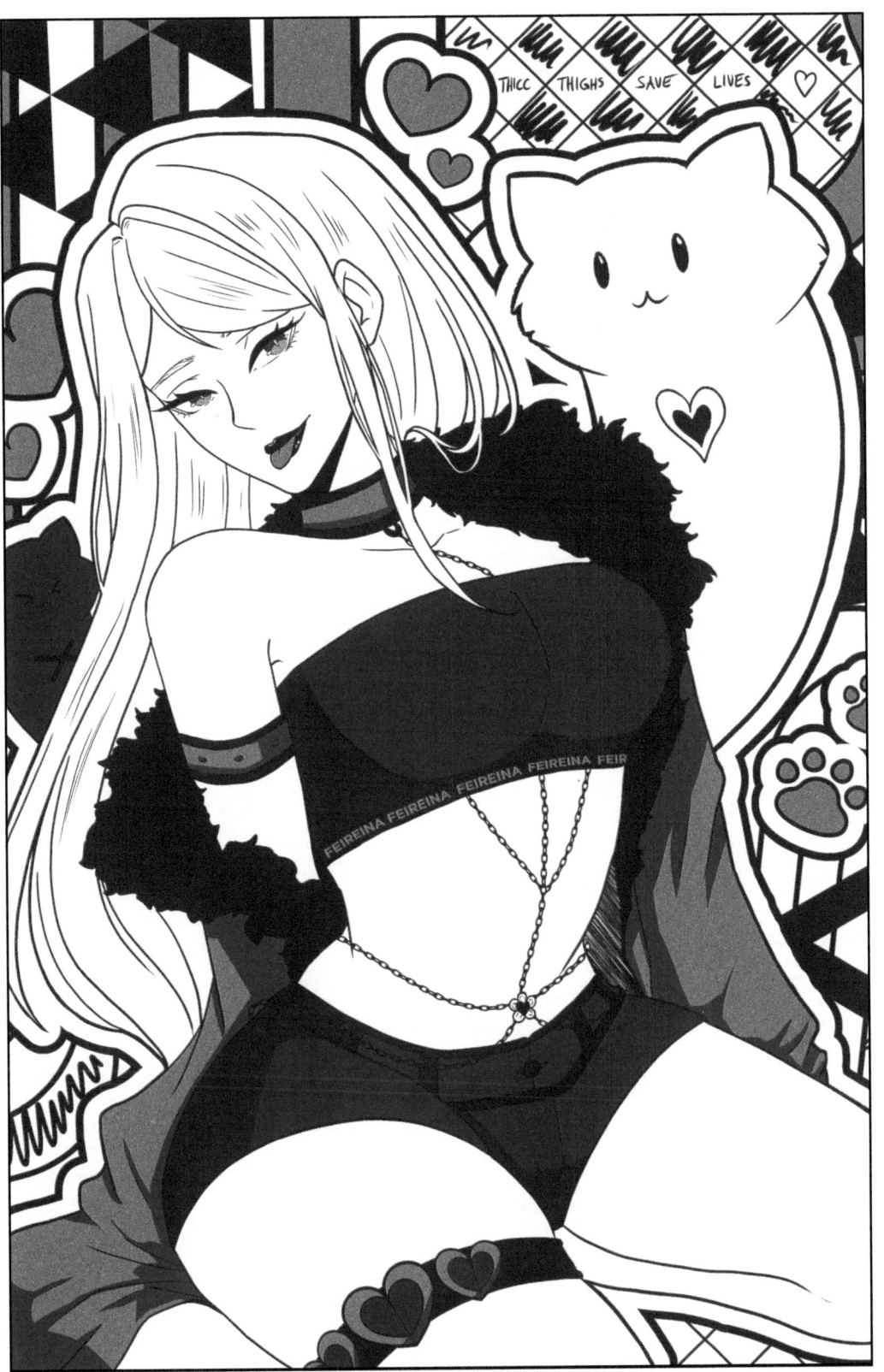

I've been challenged

This is the last guy you will see on this collection. The title is as it says. I was drawing on stream while working on this and I was having such a hard time trying to find a pose for him that won't make him look like a super twink because of the hairstyle.

And while I was sketching him out, I was explaining to chat how to make super hot guys, sharing everything that I learned from reading BL manhwas on how to make a guy look like a top.

Chat challenged me to make him one and to that I replied with "Bet."

Art Tipp:

How to draw a dude:
1. Draw the head and eyes smaller.
2. Draw the face and nose longer.
3. Draw thick eyebrows and keep it as close to the eyelid as possible.
4. Proportions are important! Make his body a Dorito!

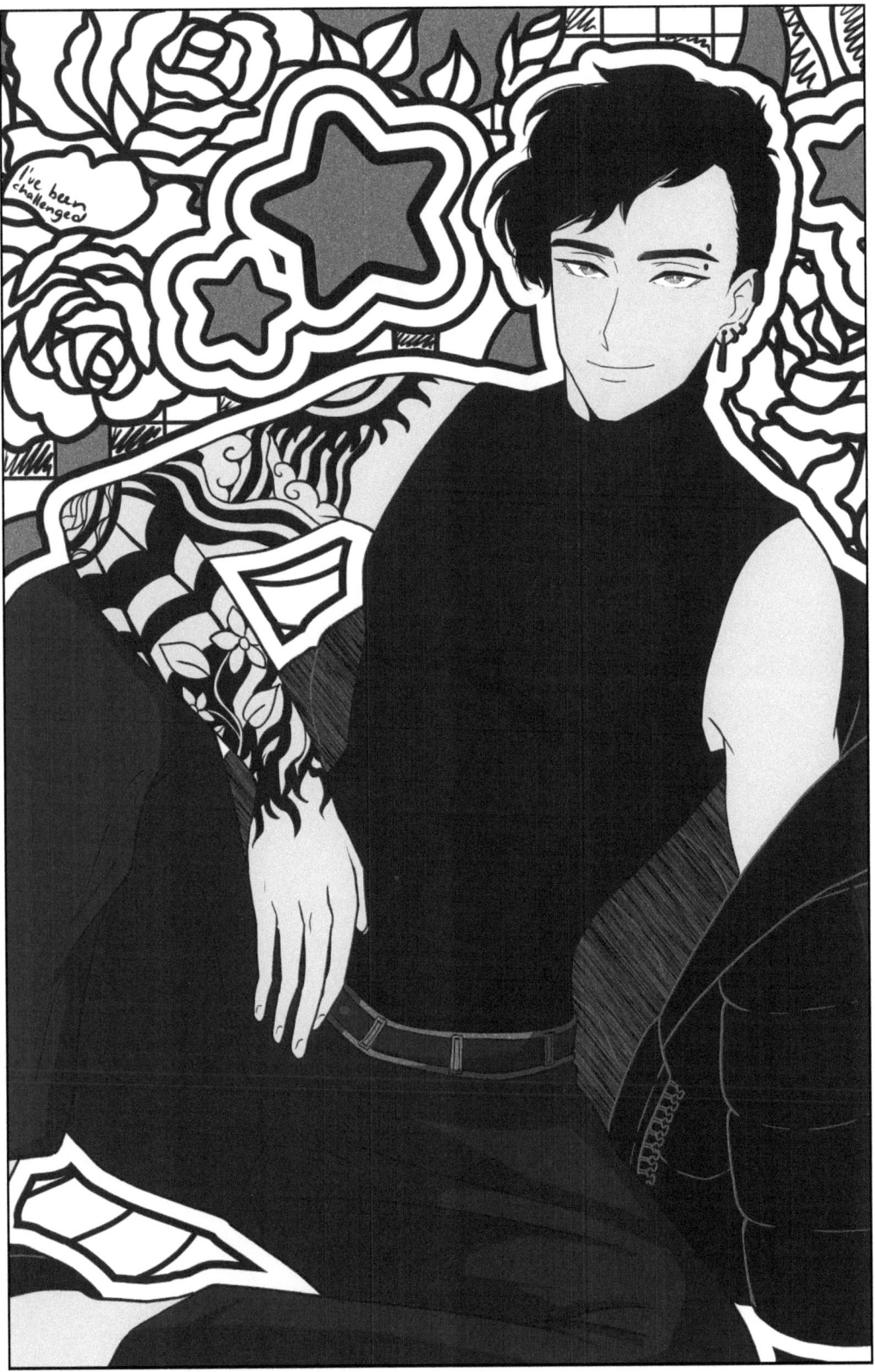

Damn I'm almost caught up!

I was so surprised when I drew this because of how fast I worked on this! I really like this pose and enjoyed drawing it alot.

I originally wanted to draw a half oni mask on her, but in the end I thought it would be more elegant looking if she wore a half mask instead. The pose doesn't show off much of what she's wearing, so I thought I really needed to add something to her thighs instead. That's why she's got those belts on her!

Totally not because I wanted to draw squishy thighs!
Who do you take me for? I'm an innocent maiden! I swear!

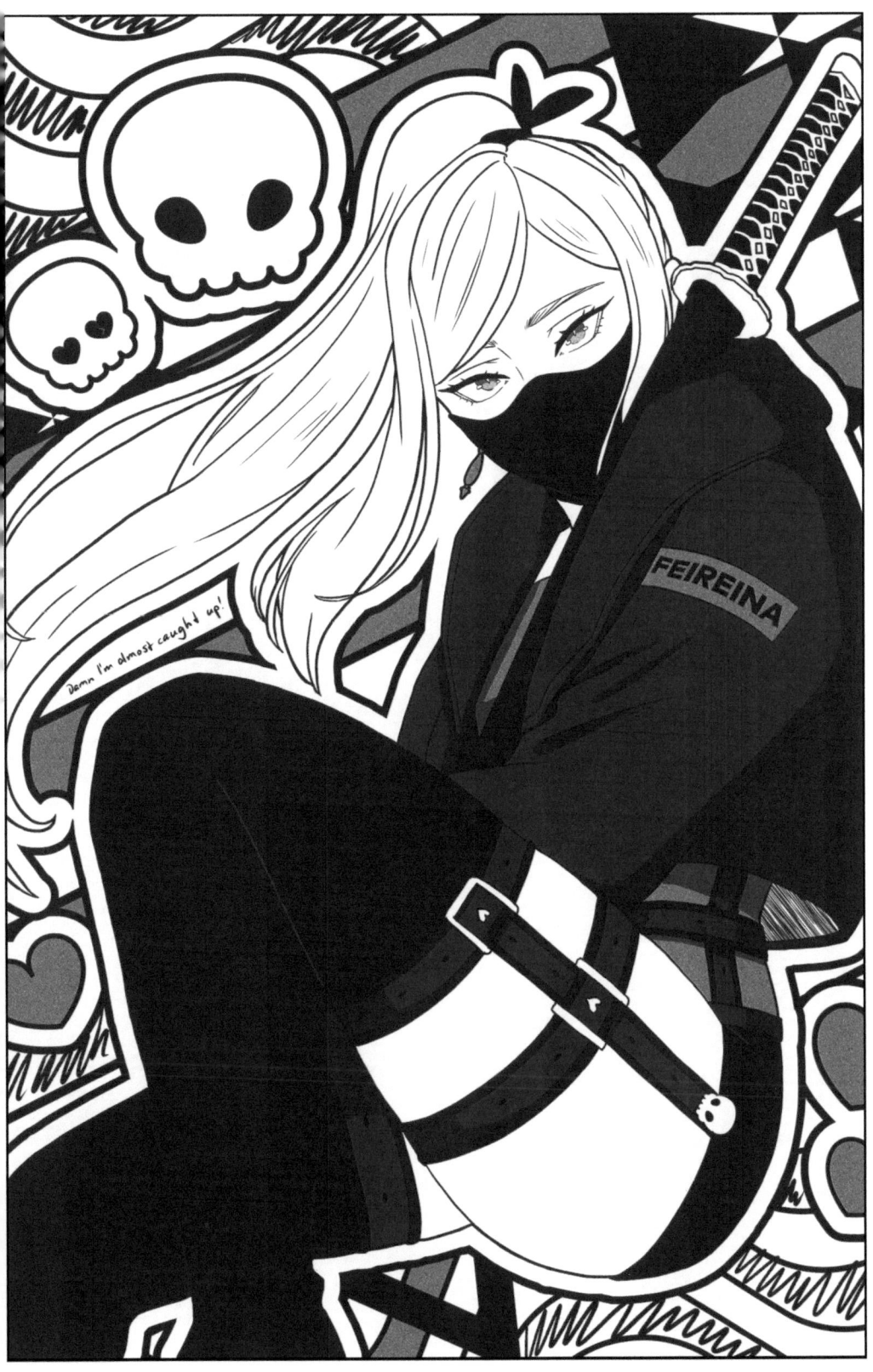

Wow! I finished the lineart in less than 2 hours!

Can you believe that? I used to struggle for 2 whole hours to even finish half of a lineart and now I can finish it in less than 2!

This piece here gave me a lot of trouble trying to find a reference for it. I wanted to give her more of a sweet vibe instead of the femme fatale ones of the previous pieces.

I actually sketched out about 5 different poses for this until I settled on this one here.

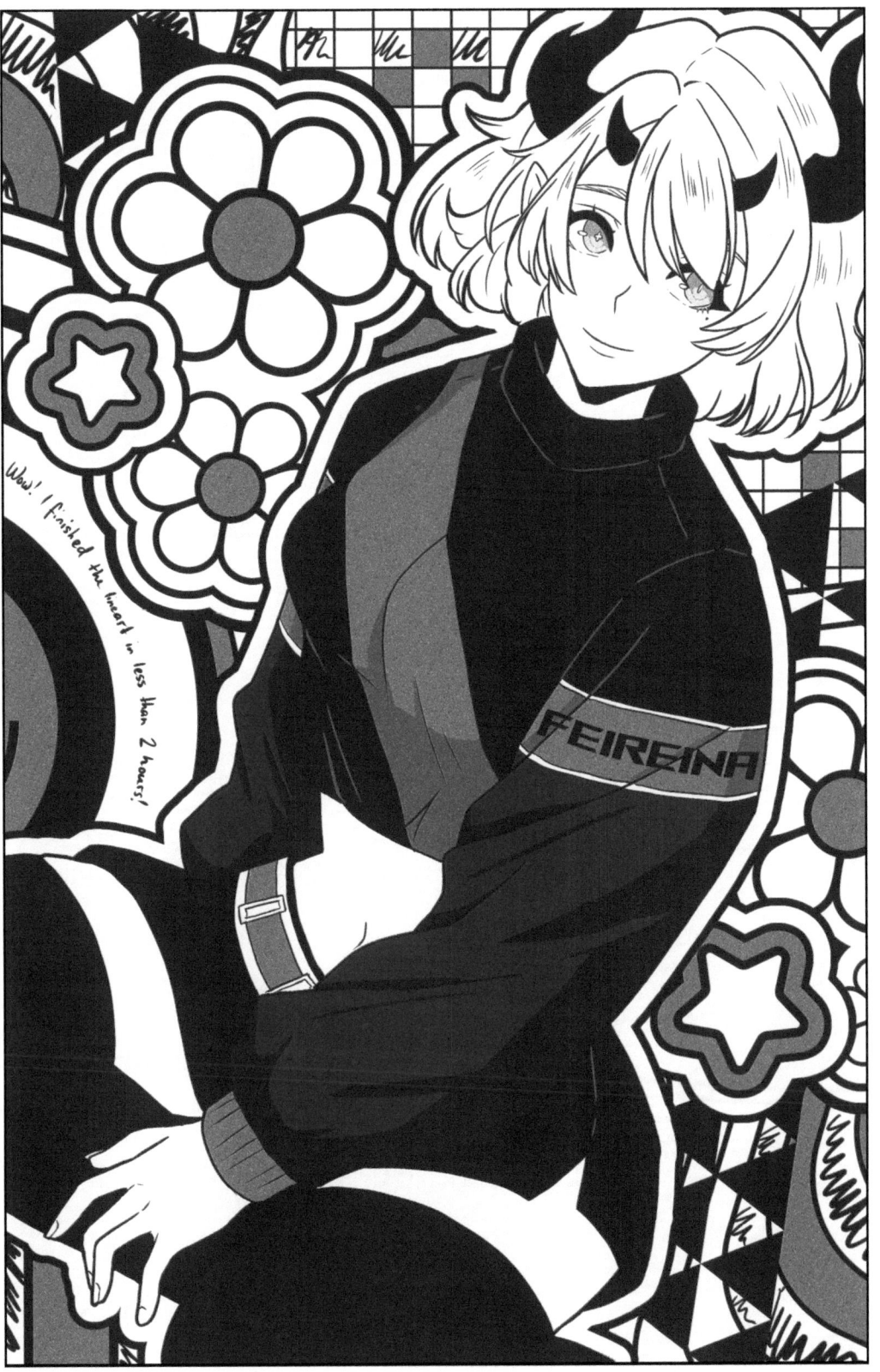

I CAUGHT UP!

Starting from this point on, I'm up to date with inktober!

This character's name is Suzu and she's also known as The Reaper because she uses a scythe to reap souls and you know what she can totally reap my soul and I'll say thank you queen.

This one was surprisingly easy to draw. Compared to a lot of my other pieces, it doesn't have as much detail, but I think it's one of the best ones I've done.

As they say, less is more. And the less clothing they have the faster I can draw.

At some point I tweeted that I enjoyed drawing the sexy ladies and someone (you know who you are) DMed me with a suggestion to start my career as an NSFW artist.

And you know what... listen.

I'm making a pin up collection! It'll be fun! But I'm not going to go full nude on that collection, it's just going to be suggestive poses ok.

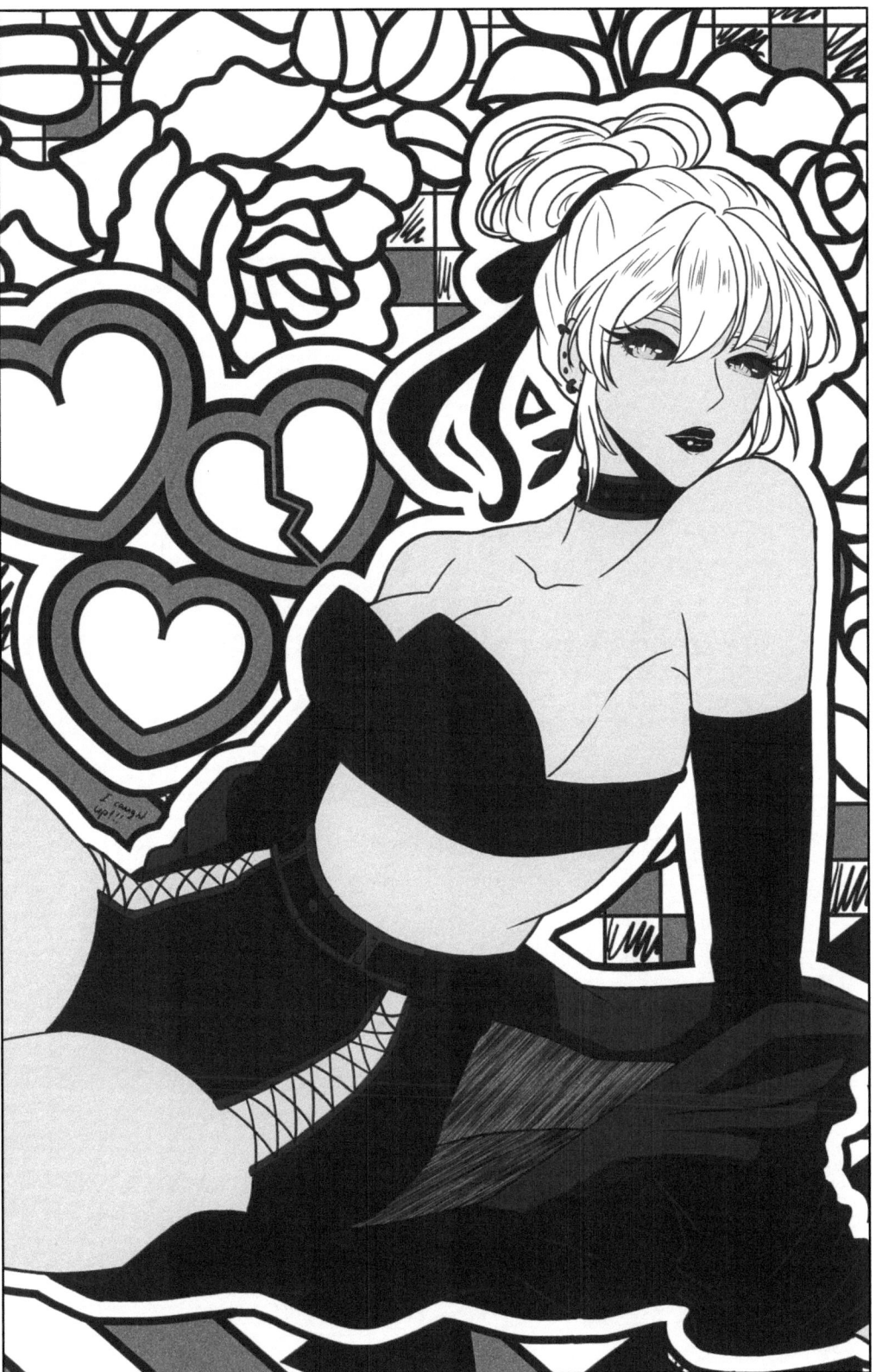

We're still on time

Okay, I posted this 1 hour after the 28th. I would have gotten it on time if my youngest sister didn't come home and we got distracted catching up and gossiping. It was fun talking to her in the bathroom! Before we knew it, it was almost 11 o' clock and we were in the bathroom for almost two hours just chatting.

Why were we having a conversation in the bathroom instead of somewhere more comfortable? It's just a girl thing. If you know, you know. You know?

This one here is a mixture of sexy and cute! I've been wanting to draw chains as a hair accessory for a while now and I finally got to do it here! Sidenote, if you want to try this kind of hairstyle out, don't. The chains will tangle in your hair and it will be really hard to take off.

Trust me I know.

I also gave her bunny thighs because uwucrew's mascot is a bunny and it's just more fitting this way!

The "m" on her necklace stands for masochist. (not morello)

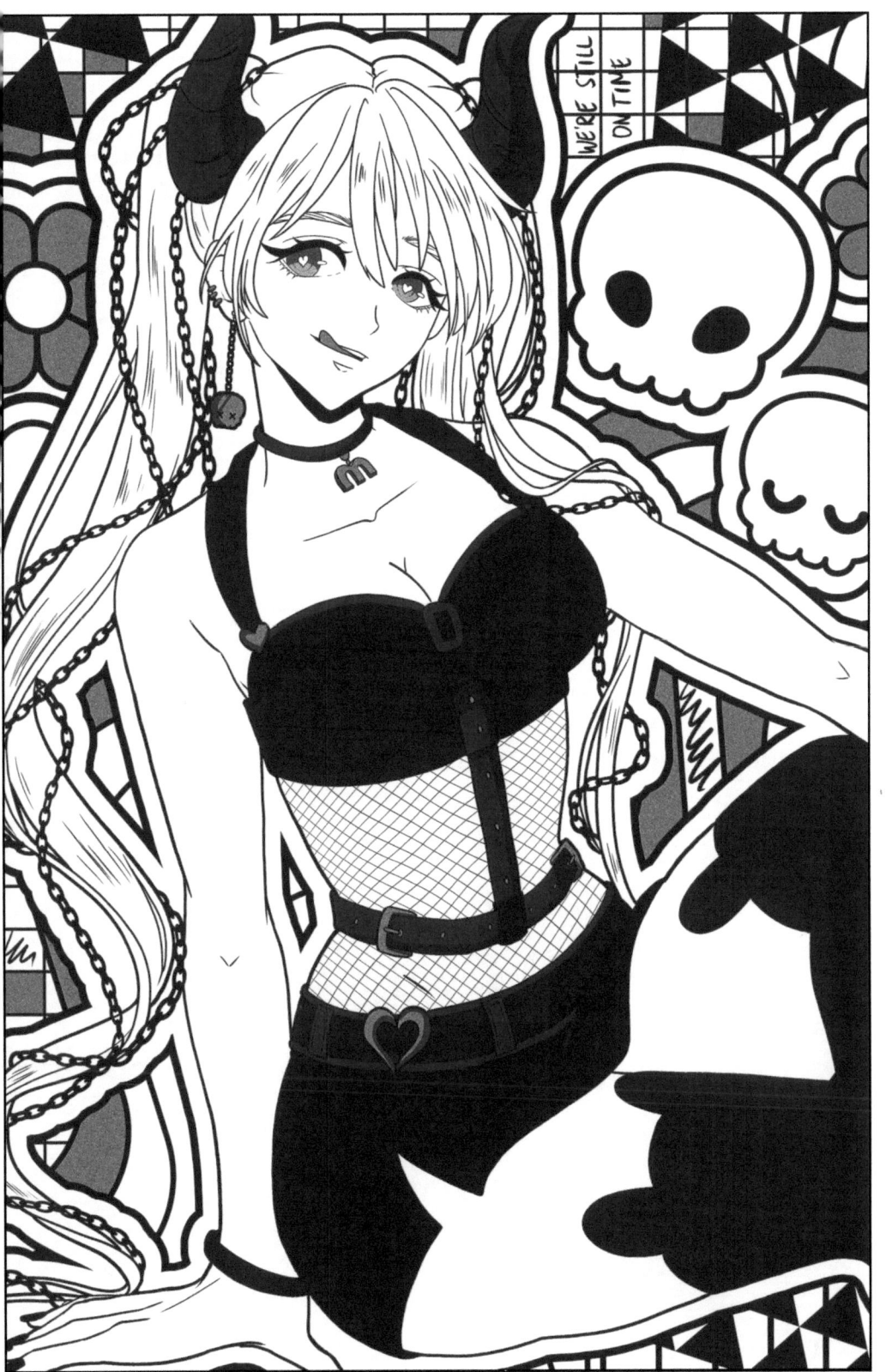

Two inktobers left to go!!!

We're almost at the end of the challenge and we got a lovely snake lady in our midst!

This is the first time I've used a scale brush and I'm very happy with the result so far! Honestly, without the shading, it just looks really weird, so the shading really made sure that the scaled don't look too unified.

I adore her expression and her forked tongue! Honestly while I was drawing this I keep holding myself back on her clothes because I didn't want it to look too mythical since everybody's clothes are modern.

Art Tipp:

Make use of textured brushes! If you use Clip Studio Paint, you have a whole gallery of free brushes and 3d models in their asset store! Make use of them! It's not cheating when even professionals use them.

Just make sure that you still know your fundamentals so the perspective and shading won't look funky.

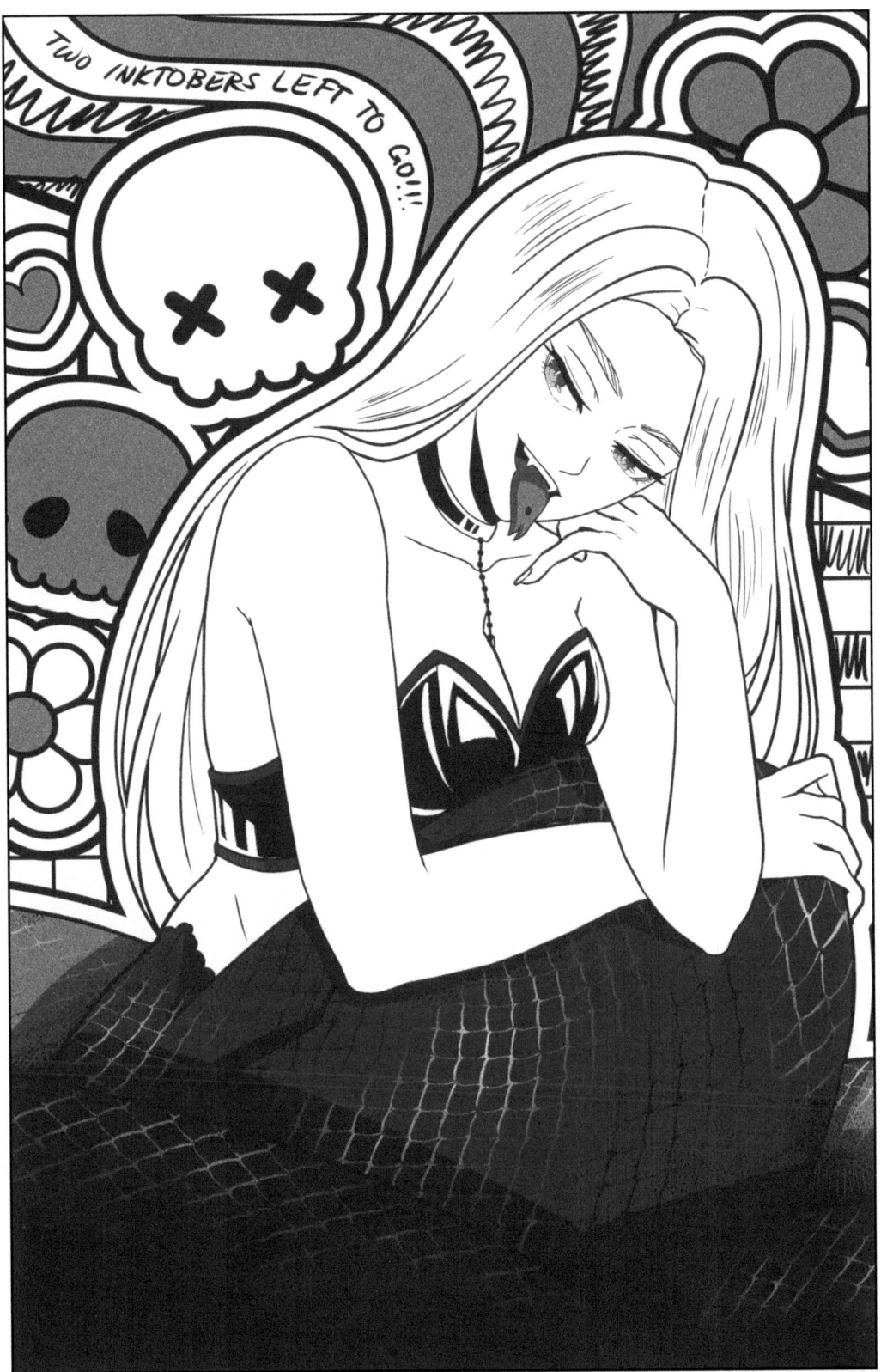

People want me to start a pin-up collection

I'm having way too much fun drawing all these sexy ladies. So I created a poll on twitter asking if I should create a pin-up collection. Most of the people answered "Yes", there was a single "No" and there were a couple of "Maybe".

Also while I was streaming on twitch, I kept getting distracted while I was doing the lineart and I was still surprised when I finished it on time!

I wanted to do something a bit more "risque" on this piece because this character is often drawn by PausePlayed in very provocative clothing and poses. So I thought "You know what let's honor her sexyness with this piece."

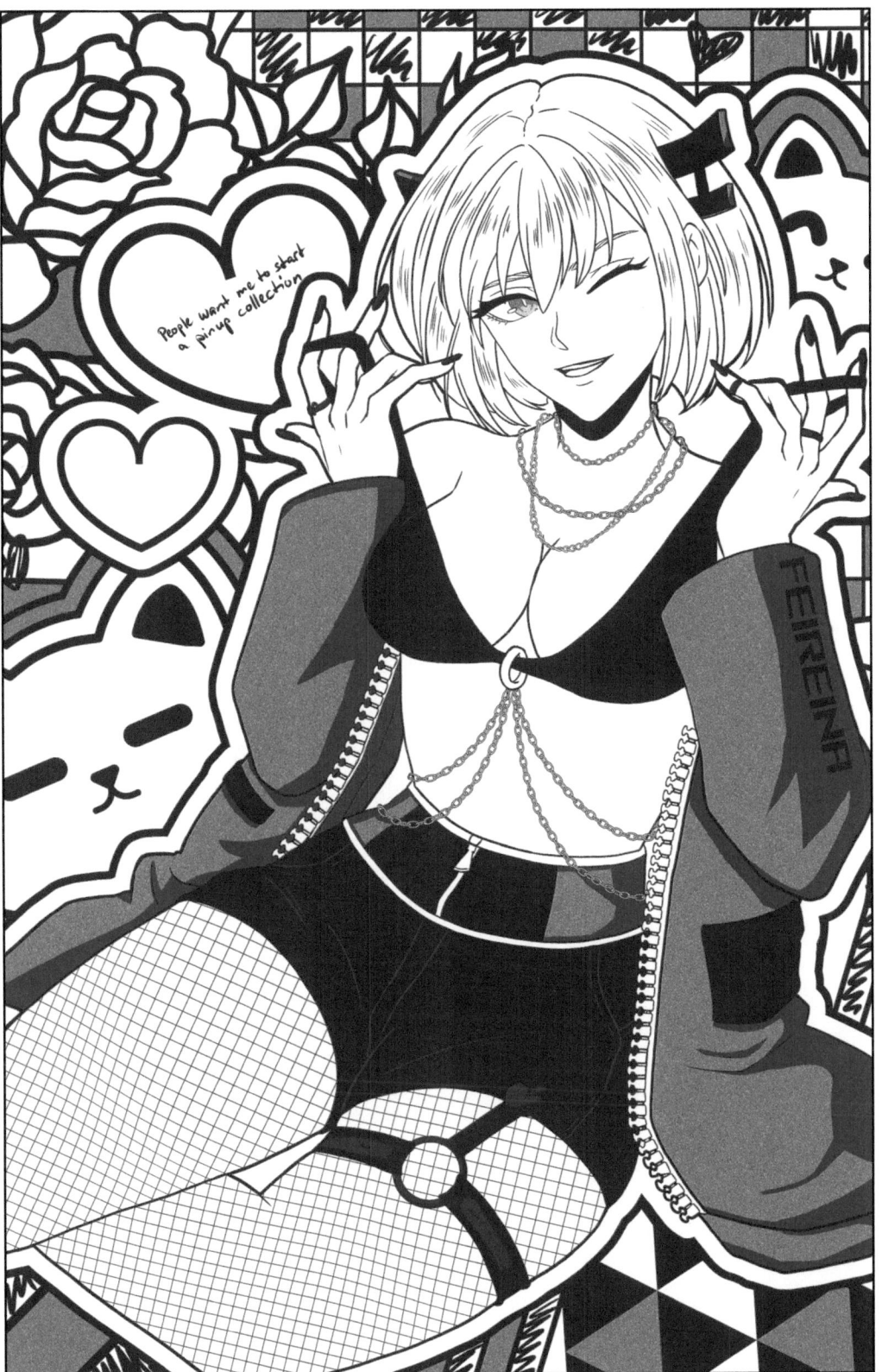

OMR Y DID YOU COME ON STREAM??

I wanted to play a small prank on him, because a couple weeks while I was working on the series, he asked to be last, saying the best is always last and all that. I told him "Okay, but I'll draw you a stick figure."

I wanted to post a stick figure on the last day, and on november I'll post the actual illustration. But while I was telling creepy stories on stream, he suddenly popped in and saw the illustration, so my little prank was ruined.

Granted it was my fault for promoting my stream on twitter, but usually he's too busy to stop by or is sleeping. Still it was nice of him to check my stream again and watch the ads.

Also he pretty much convinced me to use this illustration as the cover because it's the hottest and will definitely catch several eyes. So if you bought this because of the cover, say thanks to omr.

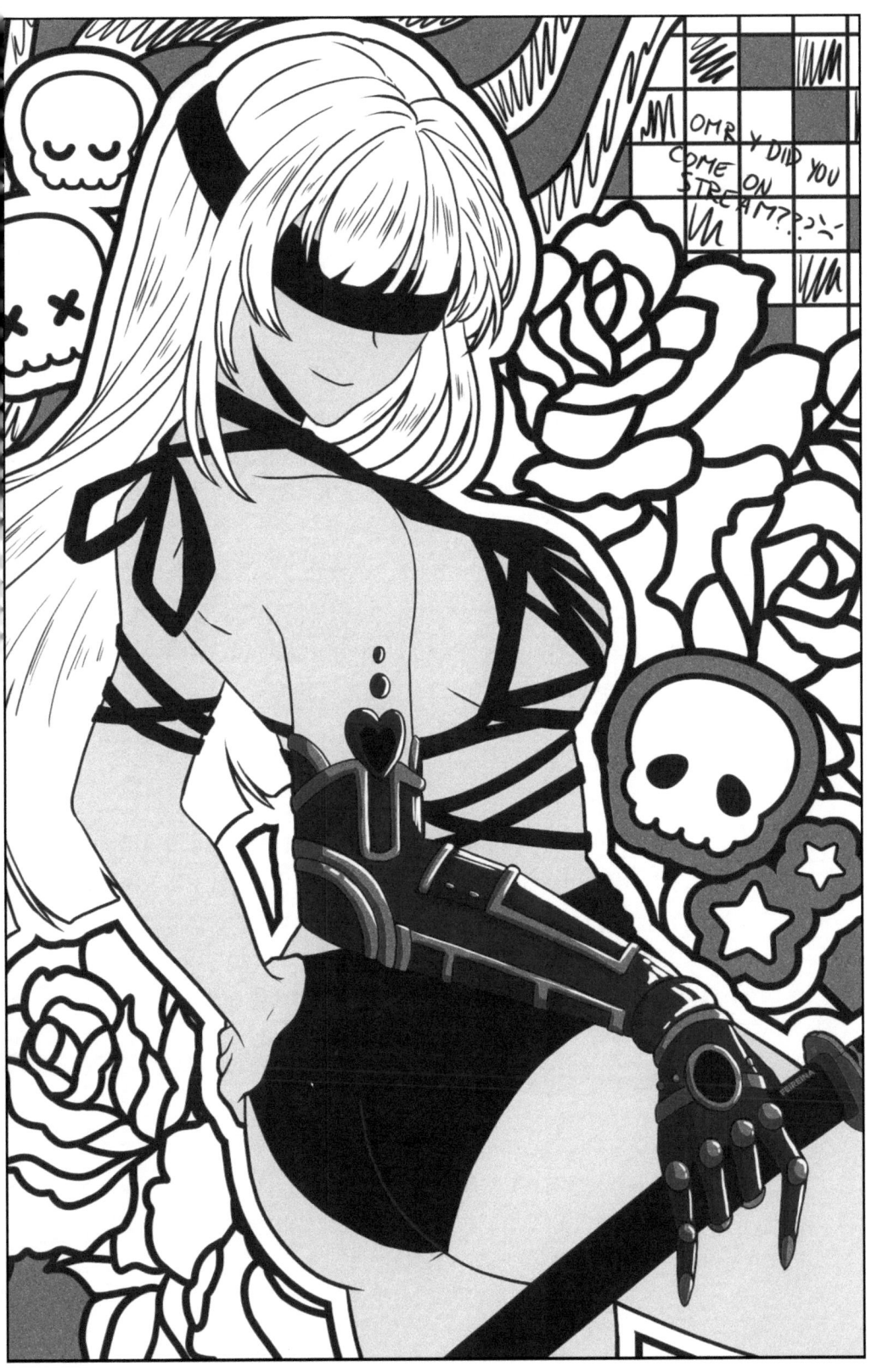

Closing words

Wow, you made it this far! Maybe you just skimmed it and looked at the pictures, but I still appreciate you getting to this page!

This was not my first inktober, nor is it the first time that I cleared this challenge. The first time was back in 2017 when I was extremely obsessed with Yuri on Ice.

It was my hyperfixation and because of that I decided to draw Viktor Nikiforov ice skating. Half way through that inktober, I wanted to give up, but my mutuals on twitter kept urging me to finish it.

That is the reason why I completed inktober 2017.

Afterwards I tried to do inktober again, but with a random theme of things I liked, which was Dragon Nest (I still love that game), Tales of Zestiria and Yuri on Ice. I didn't get very far with 2018's inktober and ever since then I decided I did not want to put myself through the stress of inktober again. After all it's hard to do when you have a job.

But here I am with my second time clearing inktober and I'm so proud! I think I improved a lot compared to when I started. Specially with the lineart! It got so much smoother in the end and I don't dread starting lineart anymore.

Apropos lineart, they're available on my Ko-Fi and Patreon shops! Just scan the QR Code at the first page and it will lead you to <u>feireina.carrd.co</u> where you can also see some of my coloured illustrations!

Now that's out of the way, the next spread I will give you some advice of what I learned while doing inktober! I hope they're helpful to you somehow!

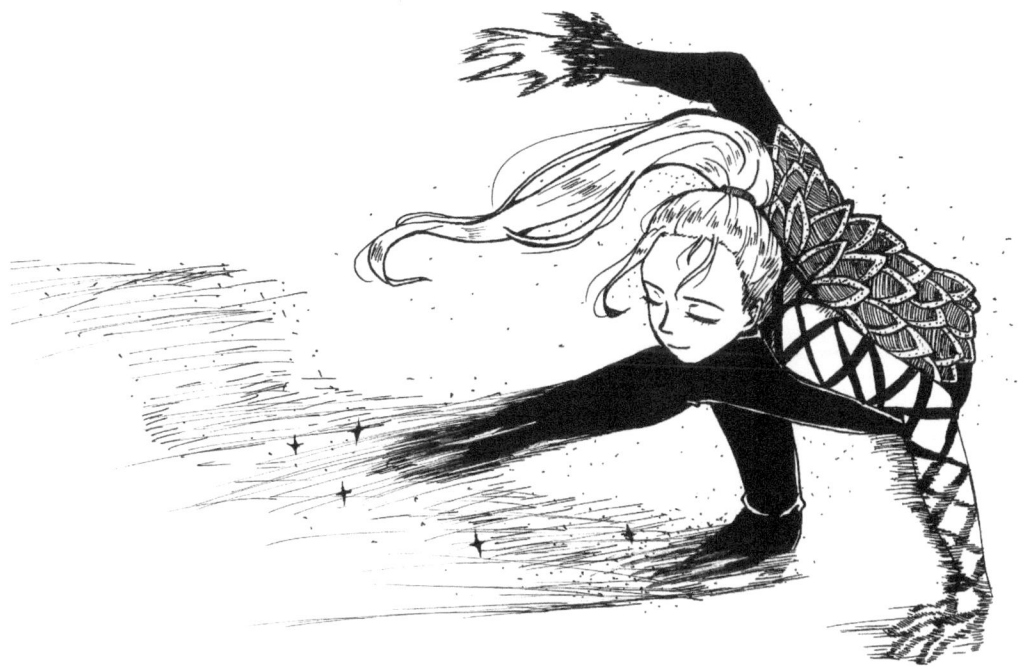

Some advice

Time

Figure out how much time you can dedicate to this challenge! I'm a full time artist now, so I could dedicate most of my time to inktober. But back in 2017, I had a job where I could only draw for a couple hours and doing the challenge made it tiring for me because all I wanted to do was get some rest after work.

Schedule ahead

This was something I learned already from my previous inktobers, but scheduling your sketches ahead of time will help you so much in clearing this challenge without having to sacrifice your social life. That being said, if you're like me, you might sketch something and decide you hated it so you start from scratch again. But at least you got the idea ready!

Details

Once you've figured out how much time you want to spend on the challenge, make sure the artworks you create are something you can be proud of to the point you can use them as part of your portfolio. For me, I realised that whenever I failed inktober, it was because the artworks I was creating weren't something I truly liked. It was just something drawn for the sake of the challenge.

Draw for others

I started out my inktober with my own characters, but as I continued on, I realised how much more fun it would be if I involved others with the project. I asked around if I can draw their OC's and because of that, I pushed through inktober and gave it my all on every single piece. I viewed it as a promise to draw their character.

Have a theme

The official inktober site always has a prompt for you to use as inspiration, but I personally don't like them all that much. What I like to do instead is to focus on a theme and something I want to improve in. In this case it's modern clothes because I rarely draw characters in modern day settings. I made a list and used it as a guide.

Add texture

If you're a digital artist like me who struggled so much with lineart, I would suggest adding a noise layer when you're working. Draw the lineart in gray so you can see the overlayed noise. For some reason, my brain likes it better when I can see textures on my tablet compared to just super smooth lines. Perhaps it's because I have a background in traditional art too and that's why my brain enjoys seeing textures.

www.ingramcontent.com/pod-product-compliance
Lightning Source LLC
Chambersburg PA
CBHW050811290526
45792CB00001B/75